# Taking Every Thought Captive

## A Guided Journal

### C. E. White

*Taking Every Thought Captive: A Guided Journal*

by C.E. White

Copyright © 2025 by Connie E. White

All rights reserved. This book or any portion thereof may not be reproduced or used in any manner whatsoever without the express written permission of the publisher except for the use of brief quotations in a book review.

Scripture quotations were taken from one of the following translations:
Scripture quotations taken from the (NASB®) New American Standard Bible®, Copyright © 1960, 1971, 1977, 1995 by The Lockman Foundation. Used by permission. All rights reserved. lockman.org

Scripture quotations taken from the (NASB®) New American Standard Bible®, Copyright © 1960, 1971, 1977, 1995, 2020 by The Lockman Foundation. Used by permission. All rights reserved. lockman.org

Scripture quotations are from the ESV® Bible (The Holy Bible, English Standard Version®), © 2001 by Crossway, a publishing ministry of Good News Publishers. Used by permission. All rights reserved. The ESV text may not be quoted in any publication made available to the public by a Creative Commons license. The ESV may not be translated in whole or in part into any other language."

ISBN: 979-8-9850311-8-8

Cover design by Jenneth Leed
Interior Layout by Jodi McPhee

cewhitebooks@gmail.com
www.cewhitebooks.com
www.facebook.com/cewhitebooks
www.instagram.com/cewhitebooks

First Edition: March 2025

Printed in the United States

*To Kourtney—*

*Without you, this book likely wouldn't have existed for years (if ever) and certainly would've contained far too many words.*

# Table of Contents

A Note from the Author ................................................... 5

Introduction ............................................................ 9

My Negative Emotion System ............................................ 11
7 Days of Journal Pages ................................................ 16

Letting Go and Laying It at The Feet of Jesus .......................... 31
7 Days of Journal Pages ................................................ 36

Replacing Negative Thoughts with Positive Ones ........................ 51
7 Days of Journal Pages ................................................ 56

Replacing Lies with Truth .............................................. 71
7 Days of Journal Pages ................................................ 78

Exposing the Roots ..................................................... 93
7 Days of Journal Pages ................................................ 100

Spiritual Motion Sickness ............................................. 115
7 Days of Journal Pages ................................................ 122

The Small Things ...................................................... 137
7 Days of Journal Pages ................................................ 142

Living Authentic Expectations............................ 157
7 Days of Journal Pages ................................... 162

Letting Go of Our Own Agenda........................... 177
7 Days of Journal Pages ................................... 184

Living Our Purpose ........................................... 199
7 Days of Journal Pages ................................... 202

Regret vs. Godly Sorrow ..................................... 219
7 Days of Journal Pages ................................... 224

Comparison...................................................... 239
7 Days of Journal Pages ................................... 244

Wrong Metrics .................................................. 259
7 Days of Journal Pages ................................... 264

Obedience Is Freedom ...................................... 279
7 Days of Journal Pages ................................... 284

Not the End ..................................................... 299

Dear Readers,

*Taking Every Thought Captive* comes directly from my personal experience of growing spiritually, mentally, and emotionally healthier. Because my own journey is limited, so is this book. It can't address everything, and I certainly don't mean to imply it contains the only tools a person may need.

This resource is not a substitute for professional care. Therapy, counseling, and psychiatric treatment are invaluable for learning, growing, and finding the support we need.

Seeking outside perspectives and guidance isn't shameful—it's a responsible choice when you know you need help. Just like hiring a plumber is the sensible solution when you don't know how to fix a leak, finding someone qualified to help is the proper response when you don't know how to heal your mind.

My prayer is that *Taking Every Thought Captive* will be one helpful step in your journey, but please don't stop here. Take ownership of your spiritual, mental, and emotional health. Keep reading, keep learning, and seek assistance whenever you need it.

May God's truth fill your heart and mind with peace,

—Connie White

# Introduction

I'm guessing you're here because you've spent enough time feeling anxious, irritable, overwhelmed, angry, insecure, and fearful. You're ready for a change. So was I.

In these pages, we'll trace some of the methods and mindsets that reshaped my life and helped me become more spiritually, emotionally, and mentally healthy.

My goal is to share bits and pieces of how the Lord has taught and transformed me using biblical advice from my own experience, growth, and the guidance of the Holy Spirit.

The short chapters expand on key truths that changed me and the processes I used to retrain my brain to believe those truths.

The Bible gives us so many tools and so much wisdom that, when applied, produce this transformation from the inside out, but many of us never learn to apply them. No one teaches us how to "be transformed by the renewing of our minds" (Romans 12:2) or "take every thought captive to the obedience of Christ" (2 Corinthians 10:5).

I was nearly forty before I recognized how much my unrenewed, untransformed mind was affecting the rest of my life. It turns out that allowing ourselves to think unhealthy, untrue thoughts leads to feeling unhealthy, unhelpful feelings and leaves us weak and vulnerable to the world's influence.

Apparently, I once told a friend I didn't really have any strong emotions except anger. I don't remember saying that, but it sounds about right. All my negative emotions felt like anger, and even that was largely invisible. I was really good at hiding it, so everything festered like an untreated infection.

## Taking Every Thought Captive

Many of us have a default negative emotion. For some people, everything bad feels like anxiety or sadness. For me it was anger that I didn't know how to appropriately express and that masked every other negative emotion…sadness, insecurity, fear, disappointment, grief, shame, and all the rest.

Some of my negative thought patterns took years to overcome, but I no longer lie awake at night berating myself for past sins, mistakes, or dumb things I said. I'm able to forgive others more quickly rather than simmer endlessly over the ways they've let me down. I rarely grow anxious about my future, what other people think about me, or whether I'll ever be successful in a worldly sense. For the most part, I'm content, joyful, and at peace.

This journal is me sharing how I got there.

I know the daily journal pages might feel overwhelming, so I'm giving you permission to do only the bits you find most helpful or what you feel capable of each day. If you want to focus on the "negative emotion system" section, do that. If you want to focus on retraining your brain to believe truth instead of lies, do that. If you just want to read the chapters and ignore the journal pages, do that.

Take it step by step. No one becomes emotionally, mentally, and spiritually unhealthy overnight, so we can't expect the healing process to happen overnight either. It's not a one and done decision or a switch we can flip, but our mindset is not a static state. It's not hopeless; it just takes intentional emotional work, perseverance, and time.

Most of the processes and mindsets in this journal have become second nature to me, and the result is that I'm happier, more at peace, more loving, more engaged with the present, and more grateful.

I pray the same for everyone who begins this journey!

# My Negative Emotion System

Since there's a lot of nuance to this section of the daily journaling pages, I thought we'd start here.

For most of my life, I ignored my negative emotions completely, viewing them all as weakness.

If I felt mad, sad, or generally bad, I just told myself to get over it. Hard things are a part of life, and you just have to push through, right?

Wrong.

Ignoring our negative emotions just gives them more power over us; they fester like untended wounds and spread infection throughout the rest of our lives.

Before we go any further, I want to note that by "negative emotions," I don't mean that the emotions are bad or evil. I simply mean emotions that don't feel good vs. "positive emotions" which do—grief, hurt, overwhelm, insecurity, etc. vs. joy, love, peace, confidence, etc.

Negative emotions are useful and purposeful symptoms of problems that need to be worked through and true difficulties that exist, and those things don't go away just because we ignore the symptoms. Whether we take the time or not, they're still in the background, making us feel sad, mad, and generally bad.

Neglecting them just leads to poor coping skills, poor reactions to others, and discontentment.

When we're honest about the fact that we're hurt, overwhelmed, confused, afraid, disappointed, or whatever else we might be feeling in the moment, we can examine and work through that instead of allowing it to control us subconsciously. We can manage and process our emotions and begin examining the underlying problems.

## Taking Every Thought Captive

For me, ignoring those emotions caused me to overreact or slide into worse thought patterns, ruminating over any situation I couldn't fix, my own failures or the failures of others, and anything that stressed me out. I would spend days brooding, growing more depressed and angrier as time went on.

When I started trying to become more emotionally healthy, I wanted to figure out how to get out of this spiral. This system is the result.

As any new habit does, it takes some discipline on the front end, but it becomes more automatic over time. Now, I'm generally able to process my emotions without days of rumination. Things don't take over my thoughts the way they used to, and I'm also quicker at recognizing and dealing with the root causes.

So here's how my system works:

**Question 1: What emotion am I feeling?**
I know this sounds extremely basic, but at first, the answer to this question wasn't automatic for me. Since all my negative emotions felt like anger, I had to dig to discover which ones had something else beneath them. So this became my first question, and figuring it out was (for me) harder than it sounds. If you're like me in this, I recommend searching the web for some feelings lists. They're easy to find and may help you identify things you're feeling that you wouldn't have recognized otherwise.

**Question 2: Is my emotion appropriate to this situation?**
Sometimes, it's not. Sometimes, we're tired, hungry, or five people have already done something annoying today. It's not fair to boil over at the sixth. Sometimes, we're overreacting to something because of a past hurt we haven't worked through yet that prompted the same emotions. This one is harder to dissect, but worth considering.

If it's a misdirected emotion for any of these reasons, we need to spend time in prayer and let it go in this moment, continually laying it at the feet of Jesus every time our minds try to pick it back up. If we identified an old wound or unhealthy thought pattern that caused our feelings, we also need to explore how to heal and forgive from that. (We'll talk more about all of this later.)

If the emotion is appropriate in this situation, we move on to:

**Question 3**: **Is there anything productive I can do about it?**
Productive is the key word here. Telling someone off is not productive, venting inappropriately is not productive, and anything we may regret later is not productive. Sometimes, what may be productive in a situation with one person is not productive with another. If the person involved is known to be illogical, selfish, or narcissistic, addressing issues may not help, but we still need to decide on a course of action with those people. Sometimes we don't know if discussion will be productive with someone until we try. We may learn the hard way that it's not. That's not a failure; it helps us know how to handle things with them in the future and lets us know whether that person is safe and trustworthy.

If there is something productive we can do, our next step is to do it as soon as possible. Maybe we need to apologize to someone, confess something, talk to someone about how they've hurt us, or ask for a raise. It could be anything.

We lighten the burden of whatever is weighing us down by being proactive instead of shying away from it. Our feelings will almost never magically resolve if we don't do the thing.

Sometimes, there may be one thing you can do right now, but a long-term plan you need to implement to continue working on the issue. Spend some time developing that plan and how you're going to execute it.

And here's the hard part: some things aren't fixable, some people don't want to work on things, and some mistakes can't be corrected.

Using this system doesn't mean everything will get better, but it does mean you can move on without regrets, knowing you did your best with the circumstance as it currently stands. It doesn't mean we had no fault

## Taking Every Thought Captive

in the situation, but dwelling in our regret will not help either. We repent and move forward, trusting that God has forgiven us. "For the sorrow that is according to the will of God produces a repentance without regret, leading to salvation, but the sorrow of the world produces death" (2 Corinthians 7:10).

After we've done all this, the last step is always to spend time in prayer and let it go, continually laying it at the feet of Jesus every time our minds try to pick it back up.

"IGNORING OUR NEGATIVE EMOTIONS
JUST GIVES THEM MORE POWER OVER US;
THEY FESTER LIKE UNTENDED WOUNDS
AND SPREAD INFECTION THROUGHOUT
THE REST OF OUR LIVES."

Today I'm thankful for: _____
_____
_____

**Anything about today that was:**
True: _____
Honorable: _____
Pure: _____
Lovely: _____
Admirable: _____
Excellent: _____
Worthy of Praise: _____

A negative thought/lie I'm trying to retrain is: _____
_____
_____
_____

A Bible verse to teach myself the truth when that thought/lie arises is:
_____
_____
_____

A song, Bible verse, or quote I'm going to ponder throughout the day is:
_____
_____
_____

Successes, progress, or things I learned today: _____
_____
_____

**A negative emotion I battled today was:** _____

1. **Was it appropriate to the situation*?**   Yes ☐  No ☐
   (*Consider whether it was a real issue or influenced by mood, circumstance, or prior events.)
   - **If NO**, spend time in prayer and let it go, continually laying it at the feet of Jesus.
   - **If YES**, ask:
2. **Is there anything productive* I can do about it?**  Yes ☐  No ☐
   (*Consider whether it has potential to repair the issue & whether I will look back on the action with regret.)
   - **If NO**, spend time in prayer and let it go, continually laying it at the feet of Jesus.
   - **If YES**, ask:
3. What can I do, and how can I do it ASAP or implement a long-term plan?_____
   _____
   _____

4. Spend time in prayer and let it go, continually laying it at the feet of Jesus.

**My prayer for the day:** _____
_____
_____
_____

**Random things I'd like to talk about, process, or remember:** _____
_____
_____
_____

**Today I'm thankful for:** _____
_____
_____

**Anything about today that was:**
True: _____
Honorable: _____
Pure: _____
Lovely: _____
Admirable: _____
Excellent: _____
Worthy of Praise: _____

**A negative thought/lie I'm trying to retrain is:** _____
_____
_____
_____

**A Bible verse to teach myself the truth when that thought/lie arises is:**
_____
_____
_____

**A song, Bible verse, or quote I'm going to ponder throughout the day is:**
_____
_____
_____

**Successes, progress, or things I learned today:** _____
_____
_____

**A negative emotion I battled today was:** _____

1. **Was it appropriate to the situation*?**   Yes ☐  No ☐
   (*Consider whether it was a real issue or influenced by mood, circumstance, or prior events.)
   - **If NO,** spend time in prayer and let it go, continually laying it at the feet of Jesus.
   - **If YES,** ask:
2. **Is there anything productive* I can do about it?**  Yes ☐  No ☐
   (*Consider whether it has potential to repair the issue & whether I will look back on the action with regret.)
   - **If NO,** spend time in prayer and let it go, continually laying it at the feet of Jesus.
   - **If YES,** ask:
3. What can I do, and how can I do it ASAP or implement a long-term plan? _____
   _____
   _____

4. Spend time in prayer and let it go, continually laying it at the feet of Jesus.

**My prayer for the day:** _____
_____
_____
_____

**Random things I'd like to talk about, process, or remember:** _____
_____
_____
_____

Today I'm thankful for: _____
_____
_____

**Anything about today that was:**
True: _____
Honorable: _____
Pure: _____
Lovely: _____
Admirable: _____
Excellent: _____
Worthy of Praise: _____

**A negative thought/lie I'm trying to retrain is:** _____
_____
_____
_____

**A Bible verse to teach myself the truth when that thought/lie arises is:**
_____
_____
_____

**A song, Bible verse, or quote I'm going to ponder throughout the day is:**
_____
_____
_____

**Successes, progress, or things I learned today:** _____
_____
_____

**A negative emotion I battled today was:** _____

1. Was it appropriate to the situation*?   Yes ☐  No ☐
   (*Consider whether it was a real issue or influenced by mood, circumstance, or prior events.)
   - **If NO**, spend time in prayer and let it go, continually laying it at the feet of Jesus.
   - **If YES**, ask:
2. Is there anything productive* I can do about it?   Yes ☐  No ☐
   (*Consider whether it has potential to repair the issue & whether I will look back on the action with regret.)
   - **If NO**, spend time in prayer and let it go, continually laying it at the feet of Jesus.
   - **If YES**, ask:
3. What can I do, and how can I do it ASAP or implement a long-term plan? _____
   _____
   _____

4. Spend time in prayer and let it go, continually laying it at the feet of Jesus.

**My prayer for the day:** _____
_____
_____
_____

**Random things I'd like to talk about, process, or remember:** _____
_____
_____
_____

Today I'm thankful for: _____
_____
_____

**Anything about today that was:**
True: _____
Honorable: _____
Pure: _____
Lovely: _____
Admirable: _____
Excellent: _____
Worthy of Praise: _____

A negative thought/lie I'm trying to retrain is: _____
_____
_____
_____

A Bible verse to teach myself the truth when that thought/lie arises is:
_____
_____
_____

A song, Bible verse, or quote I'm going to ponder throughout the day is:
_____
_____
_____

Successes, progress, or things I learned today: _____
_____
_____

A negative emotion I battled today was: _____

1. Was it appropriate to the situation*?   Yes ☐  No ☐
   (*Consider whether it was a real issue or influenced by mood, circumstance, or prior events.)
   - If **NO**, spend time in prayer and let it go, continually laying it at the feet of Jesus.
   - If **YES**, ask:

2. Is there anything productive* I can do about it?   Yes ☐  No ☐
   (*Consider whether it has potential to repair the issue & whether I will look back on the action with regret.)
   - If **NO**, spend time in prayer and let it go, continually laying it at the feet of Jesus.
   - If **YES**, ask:

3. What can I do, and how can I do it ASAP or implement a long-term plan?_____
   _____
   _____

4. Spend time in prayer and let it go, continually laying it at the feet of Jesus.

My prayer for the day: _____
_____
_____
_____

Random things I'd like to talk about, process, or remember: _____
_____
_____
_____

**Today I'm thankful for:** _____
_____
_____

**Anything about today that was:**

True: _____

Honorable: _____

Pure: _____

Lovely: _____

Admirable: _____

Excellent: _____

Worthy of Praise: _____

**A negative thought/lie I'm trying to retrain is:** _____
_____
_____
_____

**A Bible verse to teach myself the truth when that thought/lie arises is:**
_____
_____
_____

**A song, Bible verse, or quote I'm going to ponder throughout the day is:**
_____
_____
_____

**Successes, progress, or things I learned today:** _____
_____
_____

**A negative emotion I battled today was:** _____

1. **Was it appropriate to the situation*?**   Yes ☐   No ☐
   (*Consider whether it was a real issue or influenced by mood, circumstance, or prior events.)
   - **If NO**, spend time in prayer and let it go, continually laying it at the feet of Jesus.
   - **If YES**, ask:
2. **Is there anything productive* I can do about it?**   Yes ☐   No ☐
   (*Consider whether it has potential to repair the issue & whether I will look back on the action with regret.)
   - **If NO**, spend time in prayer and let it go, continually laying it at the feet of Jesus.
   - **If YES**, ask:
3. **What can I do, and how can I do it ASAP or implement a long-term plan?** _____
   _____
   _____

4. **Spend time in prayer and let it go, continually laying it at the feet of Jesus.**

**My prayer for the day:** _____
_____
_____
_____

**Random things I'd like to talk about, process, or remember:** _____
_____
_____
_____

Today I'm thankful for: _____
_____
_____

**Anything about today that was:**
True: _____
Honorable: _____
Pure: _____
Lovely: _____
Admirable: _____
Excellent: _____
Worthy of Praise: _____

A negative thought/lie I'm trying to retrain is: _____
_____
_____
_____

A Bible verse to teach myself the truth when that thought/lie arises is:
_____
_____
_____

A song, Bible verse, or quote I'm going to ponder throughout the day is:
_____
_____
_____

Successes, progress, or things I learned today: _____
_____
_____
_____

**A negative emotion I battled today was:** _____

1. **Was it appropriate to the situation*?**   Yes ☐   No ☐
   (*Consider whether it was a real issue or influenced by mood, circumstance, or prior events.)
   - **If NO**, spend time in prayer and let it go, continually laying it at the feet of Jesus.
   - **If YES**, ask:
2. **Is there anything productive* I can do about it?**  Yes ☐  No ☐
   (*Consider whether it has potential to repair the issue & whether I will look back on the action with regret.)
   - **If NO**, spend time in prayer and let it go, continually laying it at the feet of Jesus.
   - **If YES**, ask:
3. **What can I do, and how can I do it ASAP or implement a long-term plan?** _____
   _____
   _____

4. Spend time in prayer and let it go, continually laying it at the feet of Jesus.

**My prayer for the day:** _____
_____
_____
_____

**Random things I'd like to talk about, process, or remember:** _____
_____
_____
_____

27

Today I'm thankful for: _____
_____
_____

Anything about today that was:
True: _____
Honorable: _____
Pure: _____
Lovely: _____
Admirable: _____
Excellent: _____
Worthy of Praise: _____

A negative thought/lie I'm trying to retrain is: _____
_____
_____
_____

A Bible verse to teach myself the truth when that thought/lie arises is:
_____
_____
_____

A song, Bible verse, or quote I'm going to ponder throughout the day is:
_____
_____
_____

Successes, progress, or things I learned today: _____
_____
_____

A negative emotion I battled today was: _____

1. Was it appropriate to the situation*?   Yes ☐  No ☐
   (*Consider whether it was a real issue or influenced by mood, circumstance, or prior events.)
   - **If NO**, spend time in prayer and let it go, continually laying it at the feet of Jesus.
   - **If YES**, ask:

2. Is there anything productive* I can do about it?   Yes ☐  No ☐
   (*Consider whether it has potential to repair the issue & whether I will look back on the action with regret.)
   - **If NO**, spend time in prayer and let it go, continually laying it at the feet of Jesus.
   - **If YES**, ask:

3. What can I do, and how can I do it ASAP or implement a long-term plan? _____
   _____
   _____

4. Spend time in prayer and let it go, continually laying it at the feet of Jesus.

My prayer for the day: _____
_____
_____
_____

Random things I'd like to talk about, process, or remember: _____
_____
_____
_____

## Notes

# Letting Go and Laying It at the Feet of Jesus

While giving me feedback on this project, one friend told me that the phrase, "Let it go," always frustrated her, and another said the same about "lay it at the feet of Jesus." How does one simply "let it go?" What does "lay it at the feet of Jesus" or "give it to God" really mean?

Ultimately, it's about trusting God instead of trusting ourselves, someone else, or any worldly circumstance or institution. The opposite of letting go is holding on—in other words, attempting to control.

Many of our negative emotions arise because we know we aren't in control, others aren't willing to bow to the control we're attempting to wield, or we believe the person who seems to be in control can't be trusted. None of these recognize that control is ultimately in God's hands.

Psalm 55:22 says it this way, "Cast your burden upon the Lord and He will sustain you; He will never allow the righteous to be shaken."

We must *cast...throw...fling* that burden on the Lord. When we do that, He will support and nourish us as a good father does his children. It's our own unwillingness to relinquish control of the burden that keeps us weighed down.

This kind of trust requires both intentionally letting the burden go and also giving it to God. One is incomplete without the other.

### ~ LETTING GO ~

Letting go requires that we acknowledge we aren't really in control to begin with. We must recognize that our need to trust God is total, because we can't control the turmoil anyway.

## Taking Every Thought Captive

We can't control other people nor the circumstances in our lives. Any belief that we can is, at best, temporary, and, at worst, an illusion.

The Bible tells us to seek justice, to work hard, to encourage and teach fellow believers, to teach and expect obedience from our children, and gives many other mandates about our responsibilities, but we're only expected to *control* ourselves.

I am the only person I actually have mastery over.[1]

We must accept that though we can encourage others toward good action, and we can work to create a responsible environment for ourselves and others, all of that is dependent upon many systems and people beyond our influence.

But even if everything and everyone around us is uncertain, unstable, and in chaos according to all we can see, our mandate is to trust God, follow Him, and walk in self-control.

This concept is encapsulated in the well-known *Serenity Prayer* popularly attributed to theologian Reinhold Niebuhr: "God, grant me the serenity to accept things I cannot change, courage to change things I can, and wisdom to know the difference."

### ~ GIVING IT TO GOD ~

Even if we've let something go, it doesn't naturally follow that we're trusting God with it.

We can let things go fatalistically by pretending we don't care, believing the worst is bound to happen anyway, or living in the false positivity that pretends nothing bad is possible.

Living with these mindsets will leave us either hopeless, cynical, or in denial—attitudes not intended for believers. We're told to live with purpose and hope, walking in the confidence that God has given each of

---

[1] Some versions use the word "control" when interpreting the word *hypotagē*, which means 1) the act of subjecting or 2) obedience, subjection. We are still not "controlling" the other person; they are the ones who must perform the act of subjection and the obedience. This word does not speak of "mastering" or "restraining" as the words used for self-control do.

us work to do and the ability to do it (Ephesians 2:10), and trusting that even when things seem doomed in this world, God is working and will use it for good (Romans 8:28).

As believers, cynicism and hopelessness are not for us. We're never without hope, because we know that even if we don't receive what we hope for in this life, eternity will make it infinitely—*literally* infinitely—worth it (2 Corinthians 4:17, Hebrews 11:39-40). Hope is only necessary when we don't yet have what we're hoping for; if it fails when we can't see its object, then it's lacking an essential component—faith. "Faith is the certainty of things hoped for, a proof of things not seen" (Hebrews 11:1).

And false positivity that denies evil or the possibility of negative things happening in our lives will crumble at each new struggle. At best, we'll be able to stagger through minor upheavals and continue the façade. At worst, tragedies will cause us to lose our faith and turn away from the Lord. 1 Peter 4:12 tells us not to be surprised when difficulties occur, shocked as if something strange were happening to us. It's part of life; we're simply admonished to make sure the sufferings aren't for some sin we're committing (1 Peter 4:15). If we're innocent, then we can rejoice in knowing that our souls are held by God, though we suffer undeservingly (1 Peter 4:12-19).

Faith must believe it's worth following God no matter what we see. We must be able to say, "If I perish, I perish," as Esther did (Esther 4:16), "Though He slay me, I will hope in Him," as Job did (Job 13:15), and, "Yet, not my will, but yours be done," as Jesus did with the cross looming before Him (Luke 22:42).

The only way we can truly trust God no matter what the circumstances bring is if we believe in His love, His goodness, and His promises.

I mentioned above that many of our negative emotions arise because we believe the person who seems to be in control can't be trusted.

Unfortunately, this fear isn't abated simply by believing God is the one in control; many of us have trouble trusting Him because we don't understand His character. Things we've been taught or experiences we've had may lead us to see Him as an authoritarian tyrant, a distant deity, a cruel master, an abusive father, or any number of other misperceptions.

## Taking Every Thought Captive

Discovering that God is truly loving and fully good will require un-learning any false things we believe about Him and replacing it with the truth. This isn't always a quick process, but it will eventually bring us the peace of a small child confidently relying on an adoring parent.

This still isn't pretending we will face no difficulties, but it does mean the following:

- Any discipline received is for our good to make us capable of fulfilling the purpose God's created us for, just like a good parent's discipline is meant to help children grow into responsible adults (2 Corinthians 12:7, Hebrews 12:11).
- God sees and grieves with us in our pain (Genesis 16:13, Psalm 56:8, John 11:33-35).
- God walks through all our sorrows with us (Hebrews 13:5) and comforts us (Psalm 23:4).
- Any hurt He allows will be used to greater purpose (Romans 5:8, Romans 8:28, Hebrews 12:2).

There's one more piece to trusting God—we must believe that He is capable. It doesn't matter much whether I believe He is fully good and loving if I think He is weak and unable.

For me, this is a head vs. heart issue. In my head, I truly believe God is able to do all He says, but when a problem I can't see my way through arises, I begin to get anxious, angry, irritable, and overthink about different ways I can solve (control) it.

This reveals that part of me still doesn't really believe God is in control. When I repeatedly remind myself that I do trust Him and intentionally choose to focus on that, I can give it to Him.

Like Peter, we can walk on the water as long as we're looking at Jesus and trusting Him, but if we turn our eyes back to the circumstances, we'll begin to sink in worry, anger, fear, and insecurity. Isaiah 26:3 says, "The steadfast of mind You will keep in perfect peace, because he trusts in You."

When our minds are steadfast in trusting the Lord, we can have His perfect peace even if everything around us is in chaos. Indeed, this peace is incomprehensible (Philippians 4:7) *because* everything around us is in

## Letting Go And Laying It At The Feet Of Jesus

chaos. A peace dependent upon the circumstances being peaceful would be completely understandable.

Letting go and giving it to God isn't passive resignation but an active choice to trust Him. It's about releasing the illusion of control and finding freedom in His sovereignty and love. Trusting God doesn't eliminate challenges; it gives us peace amidst them.

These days, when difficult situations come up, more and more often, I hear God's still, small voice whisper, "Do you trust me?" Most of the time, this is enough to remind me of His trustworthiness, and I'm able to stop stressing, take my eyes off the circumstance, and put them back on God. If I can't, it's time to dig into some of those roots or lies I'm acting out.

When we shift our focus from circumstances to Christ, we experience the steadfast peace only He can provide. Though this trust takes time and growth, each step deepens our reliance on His goodness and power. By letting go and trusting God, we find the peace (Philippians 4:7), freedom (Psalm 119:45), abundant life (John 10:10), and rest He promises (Matthew 11:28-30).

**Today I'm thankful for:** _____
_____
_____

**Anything about today that was:**

True: _____

Honorable: _____

Pure: _____

Lovely: _____

Admirable: _____

Excellent: _____

Worthy of Praise: _____

**A negative thought/lie I'm trying to retrain is:** _____
_____
_____
_____

**A Bible verse to teach myself the truth when that thought/lie arises is:**
_____
_____
_____

**A song, Bible verse, or quote I'm going to ponder throughout the day is:**
_____
_____
_____

**Successes, progress, or things I learned today:** _____
_____
_____

**A negative emotion I battled today was:** _____

1. Was it appropriate to the situation*?   Yes ☐  No ☐
   (*Consider whether it was a real issue or influenced by mood, circumstance, or prior events.)
   - **If NO**, spend time in prayer and let it go, continually laying it at the feet of Jesus.
   - **If YES**, ask:
2. Is there anything productive* I can do about it?  Yes ☐  No ☐
   (*Consider whether it has potential to repair the issue & whether I will look back on the action with regret.)
   - **If NO**, spend time in prayer and let it go, continually laying it at the feet of Jesus.
   - **If YES**, ask:
3. What can I do, and how can I do it ASAP or implement a long-term plan? _____
   _____
   _____

4. Spend time in prayer and let it go, continually laying it at the feet of Jesus.

**My prayer for the day:** _____
_____
_____
_____

**Random things I'd like to talk about, process, or remember:** _____
_____
_____
_____

**Today I'm thankful for:** _____
_____
_____

**Anything about today that was:**
True: _____
Honorable: _____
Pure: _____
Lovely: _____
Admirable: _____
Excellent: _____
Worthy of Praise: _____

**A negative thought/lie I'm trying to retrain is:** _____
_____
_____
_____

**A Bible verse to teach myself the truth when that thought/lie arises is:**
_____
_____
_____

**A song, Bible verse, or quote I'm going to ponder throughout the day is:**
_____
_____
_____

**Successes, progress, or things I learned today:** _____
_____
_____

**A negative emotion I battled today was:** _____

1. Was it appropriate to the situation*?   Yes ☐  No ☐
   (*Consider whether it was a real issue or influenced by mood, circumstance, or prior events.)
   - **If NO**, spend time in prayer and let it go, continually laying it at the feet of Jesus.
   - **If YES**, ask:
2. Is there anything productive* I can do about it?   Yes ☐  No ☐
   (*Consider whether it has potential to repair the issue & whether I will look back on the action with regret.)
   - **If NO**, spend time in prayer and let it go, continually laying it at the feet of Jesus.
   - **If YES**, ask:
3. What can I do, and how can I do it ASAP or implement a long-term plan?_____
   _____
   _____

4. Spend time in prayer and let it go, continually laying it at the feet of Jesus.

My prayer for the day: _____
_____
_____
_____

Random things I'd like to talk about, process, or remember: _____
_____
_____
_____

Today I'm thankful for: _____
_____
_____

**Anything about today that was:**
True: _____
Honorable: _____
Pure: _____
Lovely: _____
Admirable: _____
Excellent: _____
Worthy of Praise: _____

A negative thought/lie I'm trying to retrain is: ____
_____
_____
_____

A Bible verse to teach myself the truth when that thought/lie arises is:
_____
_____
_____

A song, Bible verse, or quote I'm going to ponder throughout the day is:
_____
_____
_____

Successes, progress, or things I learned today: _____
_____
_____

A negative emotion I battled today was: _____

1. Was it appropriate to the situation*?    Yes ☐  No ☐
   (*Consider whether it was a real issue or influenced by mood, circumstance, or prior events.)
   - **If NO**, spend time in prayer and let it go, continually laying it at the feet of Jesus.
   - **If YES**, ask:
2. Is there anything productive* I can do about it?  Yes ☐  No ☐
   (*Consider whether it has potential to repair the issue & whether I will look back on the action with regret.)
   - **If NO**, spend time in prayer and let it go, continually laying it at the feet of Jesus.
   - **If YES**, ask:
3. What can I do, and how can I do it ASAP or implement a long-term plan?_____
   _____
   _____

4. Spend time in prayer and let it go, continually laying it at the feet of Jesus.

My prayer for the day: _____
_____
_____
_____

Random things I'd like to talk about, process, or remember: _____
_____
_____
_____

**Today I'm thankful for:** _____
_____
_____

**Anything about today that was:**
True: _____
Honorable: _____
Pure: _____
Lovely: _____
Admirable: _____
Excellent: _____
Worthy of Praise: _____

**A negative thought/lie I'm trying to retrain is:** _____
_____
_____
_____

**A Bible verse to teach myself the truth when that thought/lie arises is:**
_____
_____
_____

**A song, Bible verse, or quote I'm going to ponder throughout the day is:**
_____
_____
_____

**Successes, progress, or things I learned today:** _____
_____
_____

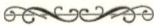

A negative emotion I battled today was: _____

1. Was it appropriate to the situation*?   Yes ☐  No ☐
   (*Consider whether it was a real issue or influenced by mood, circumstance, or prior events.)
   - **If NO**, spend time in prayer and let it go, continually laying it at the feet of Jesus.
   - **If YES**, ask:
2. Is there anything productive* I can do about it?   Yes ☐  No ☐
   (*Consider whether it has potential to repair the issue & whether I will look back on the action with regret.)
   - **If NO**, spend time in prayer and let it go, continually laying it at the feet of Jesus.
   - **If YES**, ask:
3. What can I do, and how can I do it ASAP or implement a long-term plan? _____
   _____
   _____

4. Spend time in prayer and let it go, continually laying it at the feet of Jesus.

My prayer for the day: _____
_____
_____
_____

Random things I'd like to talk about, process, or remember: _____
_____
_____
_____

43

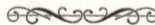

Today I'm thankful for: _____
_____
_____

Anything about today that was:
True: _____
Honorable: _____
Pure: _____
Lovely: _____
Admirable: _____
Excellent: _____
Worthy of Praise: _____

A negative thought/lie I'm trying to retrain is: _____
_____
_____
_____

A Bible verse to teach myself the truth when that thought/lie arises is:
_____
_____
_____

A song, Bible verse, or quote I'm going to ponder throughout the day is:
_____
_____
_____

Successes, progress, or things I learned today: _____
_____
_____

**A negative emotion I battled today was:** _____

1. **Was it appropriate to the situation*?**   Yes ☐ No ☐
   (*Consider whether it was a real issue or influenced by mood, circumstance, or prior events.)
   - **If NO**, spend time in prayer and let it go, continually laying it at the feet of Jesus.
   - **If YES**, ask:
2. **Is there anything productive* I can do about it?**   Yes ☐ No ☐
   (*Consider whether it has potential to repair the issue & whether I will look back on the action with regret.)
   - **If NO**, spend time in prayer and let it go, continually laying it at the feet of Jesus.
   - **If YES**, ask:
3. **What can I do, and how can I do it ASAP or implement a long-term plan?** _____
   _____
   _____

4. **Spend time in prayer and let it go, continually laying it at the feet of Jesus.**

**My prayer for the day:** _____
_____
_____
_____

**Random things I'd like to talk about, process, or remember:** _____
_____
_____
_____

Today I'm thankful for: _____
_____
_____

**Anything about today that was:**
True: _____
Honorable: _____
Pure: _____
Lovely: _____
Admirable: _____
Excellent: _____
Worthy of Praise: _____

A negative thought/lie I'm trying to retrain is: _____
_____
_____
_____

A Bible verse to teach myself the truth when that thought/lie arises is:
_____
_____
_____

A song, Bible verse, or quote I'm going to ponder throughout the day is:
_____
_____
_____

Successes, progress, or things I learned today: _____
_____
_____

A negative emotion I battled today was: _____

1. Was it appropriate to the situation*?   Yes ☐  No ☐
   (*Consider whether it was a real issue or influenced by mood, circumstance, or prior events.)
   - If **NO**, spend time in prayer and let it go, continually laying it at the feet of Jesus.
   - If **YES**, ask:
2. Is there anything productive* I can do about it?   Yes ☐  No ☐
   (*Consider whether it has potential to repair the issue & whether I will look back on the action with regret.)
   - If **NO**, spend time in prayer and let it go, continually laying it at the feet of Jesus.
   - If **YES**, ask:
3. What can I do, and how can I do it ASAP or implement a long-term plan?_____
   _____
   _____

4. Spend time in prayer and let it go, continually laying it at the feet of Jesus.

My prayer for the day: _____
_____
_____
_____

Random things I'd like to talk about, process, or remember: _____
_____
_____
_____

47

Today I'm thankful for: _____

Anything about today that was:

True: _____

Honorable: _____

Pure: _____

Lovely: _____

Admirable: _____

Excellent: _____

Worthy of Praise: _____

A negative thought/lie I'm trying to retrain is: _____

A Bible verse to teach myself the truth when that thought/lie arises is: _____

A song, Bible verse, or quote I'm going to ponder throughout the day is: _____

Successes, progress, or things I learned today: _____

**A negative emotion I battled today was:** _____

1. Was it appropriate to the situation*?   Yes ☐   No ☐
   (*Consider whether it was a real issue or influenced by mood, circumstance, or prior events.)
   - **If NO**, spend time in prayer and let it go, continually laying it at the feet of Jesus.
   - **If YES**, ask:
2. Is there anything productive* I can do about it?   Yes ☐   No ☐
   (*Consider whether it has potential to repair the issue & whether I will look back on the action with regret.)
   - **If NO**, spend time in prayer and let it go, continually laying it at the feet of Jesus.
   - **If YES**, ask:
3. What can I do, and how can I do it ASAP or implement a long-term plan? _____
   _____
   _____

4. Spend time in prayer and let it go, continually laying it at the feet of Jesus.

**My prayer for the day:** _____
_____
_____
_____

**Random things I'd like to talk about, process, or remember:** _____
_____
_____
_____

# Notes

# Replacing Negative Thoughts with Positive Ones

Most of us naturally have "negativity bias"—the unhelpful tendency to focus on the bad things in our lives to the exclusion of the good. We've all had the experience of letting five bad minutes ruin a whole day or one negative comment overshadow ten good ones.

This is human nature, but it isn't good for us. It keeps us focused on the things that are going wrong and unable to see or enjoy the things that are going right.

There are three fixes for this outlined in Philippians 4:6–9:

1) Prayer
2) Gratitude
3) Focusing on good things

Here's a condensed version of those verses (emphasis added):

"Do not be anxious about anything, but by **prayer** and with **thanksgiving** let your requests be made known to God. And the peace of God which surpasses all comprehension will guard your hearts and minds in Christ Jesus. **Whatever is true, honorable, right, pure, lovely, commendable, if there is any excellence and if anything worthy of praise, think about these things.** Practice these things, and the God of peace will be with you."

### ~ PRAYER ~

The first place we turn with any anxiety should always be the Lord. He is our only sure foundation. The daily journal closes with a place for prayer, but we've also included one here that incorporates Scripture and encourages us to remember what we know to be true (even when we don't feel it is) based on the Word of God:

*Dear God,*

*I believe You will work all things for good to those who love You (Romans 8:28)—even those things evil people intend for harm—just like You did for Joseph (Genesis 50:20) and Jesus and so many others in Your Word.*

*I believe You are fully good (Nahum 1:7), fully loving (1 John 4:16), and always working good in my heart and life even when I can't see the big picture (Isaiah 55).*

*I believe You will restore the years the locust has eaten and will bring purpose, hope, and restoration to all of my hurts, both past and present (Joel 2:25).*

*I believe You will guide me when I ask for wisdom (James 1:5).*

*I believe You're faithful to forgive the sins I confess (1 John 1:9) and remove them as far as the East is from the West (Psalm 103:12).*

*I believe that even when this world disappoints, we have a better home awaiting us in eternity that will make up for all of it (Romans 8:18).*

*I believe nothing is impossible for You (Luke 1:37).*

*I believe; help my unbelief (Mark 9:24).*

## ~ GRATITUDE ~

"Give thanks to the Lord, for he is good, for His steadfast love endures forever" (Psalm 136:1).

"I will give thanks to the Lord with my whole heart; I will recount all of your wonderful deeds" (Psalm 9:1).

The concept of gratitude in the Bible is almost always tied to reminding ourselves who God is and remembering what He's done in the past. Why? Because it bolsters our belief that He will continue being steadfast, loving, and faithful now and into the future. It reminds us of His character—that our God is unchanging, loves us, and will not abandon us.

It's right and helpful to be thankful for everything good in our lives, but our gratitude toward God is the most important because He is our only sure foundation. If the loss of any earthly good things would rattle our faith, be certain that our Enemy will do his best to take those things from us. We can see this most clearly in the story of Job. We can be grateful for those things, but we can't be reliant on them.

# Replacing Negative Thoughts With Positive Ones

Everything except the Lord is changeable, and there will always be seasons of highs and lows, abundance and loss. If we expect perpetual ease, comfort, and happiness in this life, we will be disappointed.

Nevertheless, practicing intentional thankfulness for all the good things we have helps us spotlight the positive in our lives rather than give in to our natural inclination to keep the negative on center stage—a concept that flows into the next section.

## ~ FOCUSING ON GOOD THINGS ~

"Whatever is true, honorable, right, pure, lovely, commendable, if there is any excellence and if anything worthy of praise, think about these things" (Philippians 4:8).

We have only to watch the news, scroll social media, or follow the trail of YouTube videos spiraling deeper into the horrific and infuriating to see that the world focuses more on things that are false, devious, evil, corrupt, ugly, shameful, disgraceful, and scandalous. But focusing on these things leads us to live in fear, aggravation, stress, overwhelm, anxiety, anger, and cynicism.

If we want a different outcome, we have to have different input.

The list of good things we're told to think on is sandwiched between the statements "the peace of God will guard your hearts and minds in Christ Jesus" and "the God of peace will be with you." Concentrating on these things literally protects our hearts and minds and puts us in God's presence, because God encompasses everything that is true, honorable, etc. Thinking on these things is where we find the peace that doesn't make sense to the world.

It's not about pretending that bad things don't exist or avoiding them, but those things shouldn't hold our attention or amplify our anxiety. When we're faced with the bad, the scary, or the downright evil, our action steps are to 1) bring them all to the Lord in prayer and thanksgiving, 2) take any practical steps that can impact them for good, 3) then focus our attention on the good things we see.

As an anonymous quote I saw put it, "Faith and worry both demand you believe in something you can't see. You choose." Ruminating on the negative and worrying about the future is simply the misuse of a good imagination.

Why does this matter?

When we choose prayer over anxiety, gratitude over discontentment, and hope over despair, we prove to the world that God really is our refuge, strength, and our help in trouble. We show that we really don't fear even when tragedy and chaos strikes (Psalm 46:2). We demonstrate the truth that we are focused on the unseen, eternal things rather than the visible, temporary ones (2 Corinthians 4:18). We show that we really do walk by faith and not by sight (2 Corinthians 5:7).

Our negativity bias may be natural, but it's not inevitable. God invites us to live in a way that stands out precisely because it's uncommon—a peace that doesn't make sense, a joy that flourishes even in hardship. Each time we shift our focus from what's wrong to what's right in Him, we make a profound statement: *God is bigger than all the brokenness.*

We don't ignore the darkness; we simply choose to trust God in it, spread His light, and refuse to give darkness the final word. That's the essence of faith—believing, not in the absence of trouble, but in the presence of a faithful, unchanging God who holds us through it. When we embrace that perspective, we're no longer a captive to the world's negativity, but a messenger of hope in the midst of it.

"IF WE WANT A DIFFERENT OUTCOME,
WE HAVE TO HAVE DIFFERENT INPUT."

Today I'm thankful for: _____
_____
_____

**Anything about today that was:**
True: _____
Honorable: _____
Pure: _____
Lovely: _____
Admirable: _____
Excellent: _____
Worthy of Praise: _____

A negative thought/lie I'm trying to retrain is: _____
_____
_____
_____

A Bible verse to teach myself the truth when that thought/lie arises is:
_____
_____
_____

A song, Bible verse, or quote I'm going to ponder throughout the day is:
_____
_____
_____

Successes, progress, or things I learned today: _____
_____
_____

**A negative emotion I battled today was:** _____

1. **Was it appropriate to the situation\*?**  Yes ☐  No ☐
   (*Consider whether it was a real issue or influenced by mood, circumstance, or prior events.)
   - **If NO,** spend time in prayer and let it go, continually laying it at the feet of Jesus.
   - **If YES,** ask:
2. **Is there anything productive\* I can do about it?**  Yes ☐  No ☐
   (*Consider whether it has potential to repair the issue & whether I will look back on the action with regret.)
   - **If NO,** spend time in prayer and let it go, continually laying it at the feet of Jesus.
   - **If YES,** ask:
3. **What can I do, and how can I do it ASAP or implement a long-term plan?** _____
   _____
   _____

4. **Spend time in prayer and let it go, continually laying it at the feet of Jesus.**

**My prayer for the day:** _____
_____
_____
_____

**Random things I'd like to talk about, process, or remember:** _____
_____
_____
_____

Today I'm thankful for: _____
_____
_____

Anything about today that was:
True: _____
Honorable: _____
Pure: _____
Lovely: _____
Admirable: _____
Excellent: _____
Worthy of Praise: _____

A negative thought/lie I'm trying to retrain is: _____
_____
_____
_____

A Bible verse to teach myself the truth when that thought/lie arises is:
_____
_____
_____

A song, Bible verse, or quote I'm going to ponder throughout the day is:
_____
_____
_____

Successes, progress, or things I learned today: _____
_____
_____

A negative emotion I battled today was: _____

1. Was it appropriate to the situation*?   Yes ☐  No ☐
   (*Consider whether it was a real issue or influenced by mood, circumstance, or prior events.)
   - **If NO**, spend time in prayer and let it go, continually laying it at the feet of Jesus.
   - **If YES**, ask:

2. Is there anything productive* I can do about it?   Yes ☐  No ☐
   (*Consider whether it has potential to repair the issue & whether I will look back on the action with regret.)
   - **If NO**, spend time in prayer and let it go, continually laying it at the feet of Jesus.
   - **If YES**, ask:

3. What can I do, and how can I do it ASAP or implement a long-term plan?_____
   _____
   _____

4. Spend time in prayer and let it go, continually laying it at the feet of Jesus.

My prayer for the day:_____
_____
_____
_____

Random things I'd like to talk about, process, or remember:_____
_____
_____
_____

**Today I'm thankful for:** _____
_____
_____

**Anything about today that was:**
True: _____
Honorable: _____
Pure: _____
Lovely: _____
Admirable: _____
Excellent: _____
Worthy of Praise: _____

**A negative thought/lie I'm trying to retrain is:** ____
_____
_____
_____

**A Bible verse to teach myself the truth when that thought/lie arises is:**
_____
_____
_____

**A song, Bible verse, or quote I'm going to ponder throughout the day is:**
_____
_____
_____

**Successes, progress, or things I learned today:** ____
_____
_____

**A negative emotion I battled today was:** _____

1. Was it appropriate to the situation*?   Yes ☐  No ☐
   (*Consider whether it was a real issue or influenced by mood, circumstance, or prior events.)
   - **If NO**, spend time in prayer and let it go, continually laying it at the feet of Jesus.
   - **If YES**, ask:
2. Is there anything productive* I can do about it?   Yes ☐  No ☐
   (*Consider whether it has potential to repair the issue & whether I will look back on the action with regret.)
   - **If NO**, spend time in prayer and let it go, continually laying it at the feet of Jesus.
   - **If YES**, ask:
3. What can I do, and how can I do it ASAP or implement a long-term plan? _____
   _____
   _____

4. Spend time in prayer and let it go, continually laying it at the feet of Jesus.

**My prayer for the day:** _____
_____
_____
_____

**Random things I'd like to talk about, process, or remember:** _____
_____
_____
_____

**Today I'm thankful for:** _____
_____
_____

**Anything about today that was:**
True: _____
Honorable: _____
Pure: _____
Lovely: _____
Admirable: _____
Excellent: _____
Worthy of Praise: _____

**A negative thought/lie I'm trying to retrain is:** _____
_____
_____
_____

**A Bible verse to teach myself the truth when that thought/lie arises is:**
_____
_____
_____

**A song, Bible verse, or quote I'm going to ponder throughout the day is:**
_____
_____
_____

**Successes, progress, or things I learned today:** _____
_____
_____
_____

**A negative emotion I battled today was:** _____

1. Was it appropriate to the situation*?    Yes ☐  No ☐
   (*Consider whether it was a real issue or influenced by mood, circumstance, or prior events.)
   - **If NO**, spend time in prayer and let it go, continually laying it at the feet of Jesus.
   - **If YES**, ask:
2. Is there anything productive* I can do about it?   Yes ☐  No ☐
   (*Consider whether it has potential to repair the issue & whether I will look back on the action with regret.)
   - **If NO**, spend time in prayer and let it go, continually laying it at the feet of Jesus.
   - **If YES**, ask:
3. What can I do, and how can I do it ASAP or implement a long-term plan? _____
   _____
   _____

4. Spend time in prayer and let it go, continually laying it at the feet of Jesus.

**My prayer for the day:** _____
_____
_____
_____

**Random things I'd like to talk about, process, or remember:** _____
_____
_____
_____

Today I'm thankful for: _____
_____
_____

**Anything about today that was:**
True: _____
Honorable: _____
Pure: _____
Lovely: _____
Admirable: _____
Excellent: _____
Worthy of Praise: _____

A negative thought/lie I'm trying to retrain is: _____
_____
_____
_____

A Bible verse to teach myself the truth when that thought/lie arises is:
_____
_____
_____

A song, Bible verse, or quote I'm going to ponder throughout the day is:
_____
_____
_____

Successes, progress, or things I learned today: _____
_____
_____

A negative emotion I battled today was: _____

1. Was it appropriate to the situation*?   Yes ☐  No ☐
   (*Consider whether it was a real issue or influenced by mood, circumstance, or prior events.)
   - **If NO**, spend time in prayer and let it go, continually laying it at the feet of Jesus.
   - **If YES**, ask:

2. Is there anything productive* I can do about it?  Yes ☐  No ☐
   (*Consider whether it has potential to repair the issue & whether I will look back on the action with regret.)
   - **If NO**, spend time in prayer and let it go, continually laying it at the feet of Jesus.
   - **If YES**, ask:

3. What can I do, and how can I do it ASAP or implement a long-term plan? _____
   _____
   _____

4. Spend time in prayer and let it go, continually laying it at the feet of Jesus.

My prayer for the day: _____
_____
_____
_____

Random things I'd like to talk about, process, or remember: _____
_____
_____
_____

Today I'm thankful for: _____
_____
_____

**Anything about today that was:**
True: _____
Honorable: _____
Pure: _____
Lovely: _____
Admirable: _____
Excellent: _____
Worthy of Praise: _____

**A negative thought/lie I'm trying to retrain is:** _____
_____
_____
_____

**A Bible verse to teach myself the truth when that thought/lie arises is:**
_____
_____
_____

**A song, Bible verse, or quote I'm going to ponder throughout the day is:**
_____
_____
_____

**Successes, progress, or things I learned today:** _____
_____
_____

**A negative emotion I battled today was:** _____

1. Was it appropriate to the situation*?   Yes ☐  No ☐
   (*Consider whether it was a real issue or influenced by mood, circumstance, or prior events.)
   - **If NO,** spend time in prayer and let it go, continually laying it at the feet of Jesus.
   - **If YES,** ask:
2. Is there anything productive* I can do about it?  Yes ☐  No ☐
   (*Consider whether it has potential to repair the issue & whether I will look back on the action with regret.)
   - **If NO,** spend time in prayer and let it go, continually laying it at the feet of Jesus.
   - **If YES,** ask:
3. What can I do, and how can I do it ASAP or implement a long-term plan? _____
   _____
   _____

4. Spend time in prayer and let it go, continually laying it at the feet of Jesus.

**My prayer for the day:** _____
_____
_____
_____

**Random things I'd like to talk about, process, or remember:** _____
_____
_____

Today I'm thankful for: _____
_____
_____

Anything about today that was:
True: _____
Honorable: _____
Pure: _____
Lovely: _____
Admirable: _____
Excellent: _____
Worthy of Praise: _____

A negative thought/lie I'm trying to retrain is: _____
_____
_____
_____

A Bible verse to teach myself the truth when that thought/lie arises is:
_____
_____
_____

A song, Bible verse, or quote I'm going to ponder throughout the day is:
_____
_____
_____

Successes, progress, or things I learned today: _____
_____
_____

**A negative emotion I battled today was:** _____

1. **Was it appropriate to the situation*?**   Yes ☐   No ☐
   (*Consider whether it was a real issue or influenced by mood, circumstance, or prior events.)
   - **If NO,** spend time in prayer and let it go, continually laying it at the feet of Jesus.
   - **If YES,** ask:
2. **Is there anything productive* I can do about it?**   Yes ☐   No ☐
   (*Consider whether it has potential to repair the issue & whether I will look back on the action with regret.)
   - **If NO,** spend time in prayer and let it go, continually laying it at the feet of Jesus.
   - **If YES,** ask:
3. **What can I do, and how can I do it ASAP or implement a long-term plan?** _____
   _____
   _____

4. **Spend time in prayer and let it go, continually laying it at the feet of Jesus.**

**My prayer for the day:** _____
_____
_____
_____

**Random things I'd like to talk about, process, or remember:** _____
_____
_____
_____

# Notes

# Replacing Lies with Truth

We all have internal thought patterns that have formed throughout our lives. They represent what we believe to be true about God, the world, other people, and ourselves.

I hate to break it to you, but these thought patterns are often incorrect. We believe a lot of lies—more, even, than we probably realize. We often say we believe one thing while our actions reveal that, deep down, we actually believe something else.

I may say that I believe God is good, but if I don't want to do what He says because I'm afraid of how it will impact my life, then I don't truly believe He is good. That shows that I believe—as Eve did in the very beginning (Genesis 3:1-6)—that I suspect God will withhold something good from me. I fear that what He has for me will be too difficult, too restrictive, and will not truly be the best.

But not all wrong thoughts are hidden beneath what we think we should believe; some are right out in the open. For instance, perhaps you believe you're useless and a failure. Perhaps you believe that all men are untrustworthy and unsafe. Perhaps you believe you're always a bother to those around you. Perhaps you believe no one will love you unless you act or look a certain way. Perhaps you believe you're entitled to a certain kind of life or treatment from others.

Sometimes we're unaware something we believe *is* a lie. We usually believe these things because they've been true in certain circumstances or because we've been informed and influenced by other people, our experiences, our education, society, and by our Enemy, the devil.

These often seem like reasonable sources, but they're never foolproof. All are about as consistent as Jell-o. Each new person, experience, bit of

## Taking Every Thought Captive

knowledge, or societal norm may turn our Jell-o mold of beliefs into an indistinguishable mound of mush. If we're looking for truth in these things, then our beliefs will be limited to the intelligence and opinions of the people we know or have had the privilege to learn from, the very limited experiences we've had, an extremely tiny slice of culture and knowledge based on our time and place in history, or—what's worse—an Enemy who is actively trying to deceive us.

What we think and believe is of the utmost importance, because that's what informs our emotions and actions. So if those thoughts and beliefs are untrue, they are causing us to believe and feel things that are harmfully informing our experience and our relationships.

We find the biblical answer to all this here: "Do not be conformed to this world, but **be transformed by the renewing of your mind**, so that you may prove what the will of God is, that which is good and acceptable and perfect" (Romans 12:2, emphasis added).

We cannot allow our thoughts and beliefs to conform to what the world says. We must be transformed by the renewing of our minds. Through this, we learn to see God's will for us and the world around us. This happens when we teach our minds the truth so we're no longer living false thoughts and beliefs which influence our emotions and cause all kinds of havoc in our lives.

This truth can only be found in God, His Word, and what we know of His character. There are (at least) four reasons for this.

1. **He is our Creator (Acts 17:24).** As our designer, He knows exactly what our purpose is and how we need to live in order to accomplish it (Acts 17:26, Ephesians 2:10) just like an inventor is the one most qualified to say what his machine does and how to run it. Only in God will I find the answers for my life, because only in Him do I "live and move and exist" (Acts 17:28).

2. **He is omniscient (Psalm 147:5).** Unlimited by time or space, He knows all there is to know. He is not influenced by any external input—culture, time, or experience. He's the only being

capable of complete objectivity because He knows all truth. He also cannot lie (Hebrews 6:18), so all He tells us from this unlimited knowledge must be true.

3. **He is omnipotent (Jeremiah 32:17).** He owns the cattle on a thousand hills (Psalm 50:10) and needs nothing from anyone (Acts 17:24–25), so He cannot be manipulated by desire or need.

4. **He is unchangeable (James 1:17).** No truth can be verified by something or someone constantly in flux. Our own ever-shifting thoughts, feelings, and beliefs illustrate that they're unreliable; we must rely on what the immutable God tells us.

So when I find I've been believing or living like I believe a lie (anything that counters Scripture) or I'm not walking in faith (Hebrews 11:6), I use a Bible verse as my proof text every time that lie shows up in my mind or comes out in my actions.

Here are a few examples of lies and verses I use to counter them:

**Lie 1:** "God is withholding something good from me and what He intends for my life will be too restrictive and difficult."
**Truth:**
- "For the Lord God is a sun and shield; the Lord gives grace and glory; **He withholds no good thing from those who walk with integrity**" (Psalm 84:11, emphasis added).
- "For this is the love of God, that we keep His commandments; and **His commandments are not burdensome**" (1 John 5:3, emphasis added).

**Lie 2:** "I'm useless."
**Truth:**
- "But now **God has arranged the parts, each one of them in the body, just as He desired.** If they were all one part, where would the body be? But now there are many parts, but one body. **And**

the eye cannot say to the hand, 'I have no need of you'; or again, the head to the feet, 'I have no need of you' (1 Corinthians 12:18-21, emphasis added).
- "For **we are His workmanship, created in Christ Jesus for good works, which God prepared beforehand** so that we would walk in them" (Ephesians 2:10, emphasis added).

**Lie 3:** "I'm entitled to be treated and live to a certain standard because I am _____." (This blank may be filled with any qualification—talented, attractive, moral, well-educated, wealthy, prestigious, etc.)
**Truth:**
- "Do nothing from selfishness or empty conceit, but with humility **consider one another as more important than yourselves**" (Philippians 2:3, emphasis added).
- "**Have this attitude in yourselves which was also in Christ Jesus, who, although He existed in the form of God did not regard equality with God a thing to be grasped, but emptied Himself, taking the form of a bond-servant, and being made in the likeness of men. Being found in appearance as a man, He humbled Himself by becoming obedient to the point of death, even death on a cross.** (Philippians 2:5-9, emphasis added).

If I'm battling Lie 1, tempted to go against something Jesus said because my immediate desires seem threatened and it requires I go without something my flesh believes is good, I remind myself, "No. I know that God 'withholds no good thing from those who walk in integrity.' I know that He lights my way and protects me like a sun and shield. I know that He gives me grace and glory. I want to walk in integrity and receive all the protection, grace, and glory God intends for me."

You can also associate a story that illustrates the truth in a way that helps you believe it. That's why Jesus told parables, because it brings the truth to life. For this lie, I think of the time my kitten stole a chicken wing off my plate. I chased her down, and we played tug-of-war with it. I wasn't taking it from her because I was withholding sustenance or

## Replacing Lies With Truth

because I didn't want her to have something tasty; I was taking it because I know that cooked bones can splinter and be harmful for cats. But, fresh from the shelter, this feisty three-pound fluff was absolutely certain the mean giant was trying to withhold something good from her. Nothing could have convinced her little cat brain otherwise.

Her belief was influenced by her fear that she had to take everything she could get because the next meal was never guaranteed. Her experience had led her to believe she had to fight for every bite. She didn't understand that she could trust me to provide everything she would ever need, and she's not capable of understanding that what looks good can sometimes be harmful.

I consider these things when I feel like God is withholding something from me. Perhaps I don't think I can give something up because I fear without it, I won't have enough of whatever it represents. I won't have enough love or comfort, money or ease, approval or leisure time. I haven't yet grasped that God is caring for me in ways I could never imagine, just like I care for my cat. I can trust that if it feels like withholding right now, He will fulfill that need in another way, just like I was always going to give my cat her appropriate dinner later. Letting the chicken bone go didn't mean she was going to starve. And I can believe—even when my little human brain can't conceive of why—that the thing I want may somehow be harmful for me. It is through withholding it that God is acting as my shield. He's protecting me from something that's *not* good for me in this particular circumstance and this particular time.

If you can't think of a story from your own life that combats your lie and brings the truth to life for you, search for something or ask your friends.

You also don't have to memorize the truth verse word-for-word; you can make it longer or shorter or whatever is meaningful to you.

For instance, if I'm battling Lie 3, angry because someone didn't give me the respect I deserve or because despite my hard work, ability, etc., things in my life are still difficult, I remind myself, "No. I want to have the same attitude Christ did. He was God Himself, completely perfect, and deserved to be served and worshipped, yet He willingly humbled himself, served others, gave up those rights, lived immeasurably far below what He deserved, and was killed unjustly. So I can live a life of love, purpose, contentment, and humility even when I'm mistreated and living in difficulty."

The way I stated this is important. We often think that accepting mistreatment, not getting what we deserve, or living through lack with grace, patience, and contentment means we must also believe that we *deserve* to be mistreated and to not receive good things. We can see that's not the case; Jesus deserved all the good things this world had to offer, yet did not require or expect them, choosing instead to be a servant and live for others. It's not that we don't have rights; it's that we choose to live life humbly, sacrificially, and in love just like Christ did, even as His rights were violated.

When I'm working to renew my mind and be transformed by replacing a lie I've internalized, I speak the truth back to my mind like this every time I think the lie or the evidence of my belief in the lie comes out in my actions. And when I say every time, I mean I might have to do it over and over and over again many times a day…or an hour…depending on which lie I'm battling.

Our brains have old habits, and we must retrain them (renew our minds) so we'll be transformed from the inside out. It takes discipline. I won't pretend it's easy. It's tiring, and it requires intentional work and effort.

But what I know after retraining many embedded lies is that *it works*. I am being transformed. Most of my lies only took a few months to stop popping into my head or out into my actions unbidden. Some have taken longer than others, but as time goes on, even those appear less often and usually begin to have less of an emotional hold on me when they do appear. They feel not so much like my actual feelings and beliefs but like it does when you accidentally turn the wrong direction toward somewhere you used to live. It was an automatic action, but it doesn't indicate where you really want to go. When it happens, it doesn't derail you; you just turn around and go back the other way.

## Replacing Lies With Truth

My advice is to start with one thought at a time—maybe two if it doesn't seem overwhelming. As you're filling out the daily journal, feel free to write the same thing in the "negative thought/lie I'm retraining" blank every day for months if you need to. Pick the lie that's causing you the most trouble, then find a Bible verse that speaks truth into it—something that's meaningful to you. Ask the Lord to help you notice when you're feeling and acting out of that lie. When it pops up, tell yourself the truth and repent of believing the lie. Do it every time. As the process begins to feel more natural and you begin to gain freedom for one lie, add another that needs to be retrained.

Transformation will come!

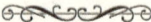

**Today I'm thankful for:** _____
_____
_____

**Anything about today that was:**
True: _____
Honorable: _____
Pure: _____
Lovely: _____
Admirable: _____
Excellent: _____
Worthy of Praise: _____

**A negative thought/lie I'm trying to retrain is:** _____
_____
_____
_____

**A Bible verse to teach myself the truth when that thought/lie arises is:**
_____
_____
_____

**A song, Bible verse, or quote I'm going to ponder throughout the day is:**
_____
_____
_____

**Successes, progress, or things I learned today:** _____
_____
_____

**A negative emotion I battled today was:** _____

1. **Was it appropriate to the situation*?**   Yes ☐  No ☐
   (*Consider whether it was a real issue or influenced by mood, circumstance, or prior events.)
   - **If NO**, spend time in prayer and let it go, continually laying it at the feet of Jesus.
   - **If YES**, ask:
2. **Is there anything productive* I can do about it?**   Yes ☐  No ☐
   (*Consider whether it has potential to repair the issue & whether I will look back on the action with regret.)
   - **If NO**, spend time in prayer and let it go, continually laying it at the feet of Jesus.
   - **If YES**, ask:
3. What can I do, and how can I do it ASAP or implement a long-term plan? _____
   _____
   _____

4. Spend time in prayer and let it go, continually laying it at the feet of Jesus.

**My prayer for the day:** _____
_____
_____
_____

**Random things I'd like to talk about, process, or remember:** _____
_____
_____
_____

Today I'm thankful for: _____
_____
_____

**Anything about today that was:**
True: _____
Honorable: _____
Pure: _____
Lovely: _____
Admirable: _____
Excellent: _____
Worthy of Praise: _____

A negative thought/lie I'm trying to retrain is: _____
_____
_____
_____

A Bible verse to teach myself the truth when that thought/lie arises is:
_____
_____
_____

A song, Bible verse, or quote I'm going to ponder throughout the day is:
_____
_____
_____

Successes, progress, or things I learned today: _____
_____
_____

**A negative emotion I battled today was:** _____

1. **Was it appropriate to the situation*?** Yes ☐ No ☐
   (*Consider whether it was a real issue or influenced by mood, circumstance, or prior events.)
   - **If NO**, spend time in prayer and let it go, continually laying it at the feet of Jesus.
   - **If YES**, ask:
2. **Is there anything productive* I can do about it?** Yes ☐ No ☐
   (*Consider whether it has potential to repair the issue & whether I will look back on the action with regret.)
   - **If NO**, spend time in prayer and let it go, continually laying it at the feet of Jesus.
   - **If YES**, ask:
3. **What can I do, and how can I do it ASAP or implement a long-term plan?** _____
   _____
   _____

4. **Spend time in prayer and let it go, continually laying it at the feet of Jesus.**

**My prayer for the day:** _____
_____
_____
_____

**Random things I'd like to talk about, process, or remember:** _____
_____
_____
_____

Today I'm thankful for: _____
_____
_____

**Anything about today that was:**
True: _____
Honorable: _____
Pure: _____
Lovely: _____
Admirable: _____
Excellent: _____
Worthy of Praise: _____

A negative thought/lie I'm trying to retrain is: _____
_____
_____
_____

A Bible verse to teach myself the truth when that thought/lie arises is:
_____
_____
_____

A song, Bible verse, or quote I'm going to ponder throughout the day is:
_____
_____
_____

Successes, progress, or things I learned today: _____
_____
_____

A negative emotion I battled today was: _____

1. Was it appropriate to the situation*?   Yes ☐  No ☐
   (*Consider whether it was a real issue or influenced by mood, circumstance, or prior events.)
   - **If NO**, spend time in prayer and let it go, continually laying it at the feet of Jesus.
   - **If YES**, ask:
2. Is there anything productive* I can do about it?  Yes ☐  No ☐
   (*Consider whether it has potential to repair the issue & whether I will look back on the action with regret.)
   - **If NO**, spend time in prayer and let it go, continually laying it at the feet of Jesus.
   - **If YES**, ask:
3. What can I do, and how can I do it ASAP or implement a long-term plan? _____
   _____
   _____

4. Spend time in prayer and let it go, continually laying it at the feet of Jesus.

My prayer for the day: _____
_____
_____
_____

Random things I'd like to talk about, process, or remember: _____
_____
_____

Today I'm thankful for: _____

_____

_____

**Anything about today that was:**

True: _____

Honorable: _____

Pure: _____

Lovely: _____

Admirable: _____

Excellent: _____

Worthy of Praise: _____

**A negative thought/lie I'm trying to retrain is:** _____

_____

_____

_____

**A Bible verse to teach myself the truth when that thought/lie arises is:**

_____

_____

_____

**A song, Bible verse, or quote I'm going to ponder throughout the day is:**

_____

_____

_____

**Successes, progress, or things I learned today:** _____

_____

_____

**A negative emotion I battled today was:** _____

1. **Was it appropriate to the situation*?**   Yes ☐  No ☐
   (*Consider whether it was a real issue or influenced by mood, circumstance, or prior events.)
   - **If NO**, spend time in prayer and let it go, continually laying it at the feet of Jesus.
   - **If YES**, ask:
2. **Is there anything productive* I can do about it?**  Yes ☐  No ☐
   (*Consider whether it has potential to repair the issue & whether I will look back on the action with regret.)
   - **If NO**, spend time in prayer and let it go, continually laying it at the feet of Jesus.
   - **If YES**, ask:
3. **What can I do, and how can I do it ASAP or implement a long-term plan?** _____
   _____
   _____

4. **Spend time in prayer and let it go, continually laying it at the feet of Jesus.**

**My prayer for the day:** _____
_____
_____
_____

**Random things I'd like to talk about, process, or remember:** _____
_____
_____
_____

Today I'm thankful for: _____
_____
_____

**Anything about today that was:**
True: _____
Honorable: _____
Pure: _____
Lovely: _____
Admirable: _____
Excellent: _____
Worthy of Praise: _____

A negative thought/lie I'm trying to retrain is: _____
_____
_____
_____

A Bible verse to teach myself the truth when that thought/lie arises is:
_____
_____
_____

A song, Bible verse, or quote I'm going to ponder throughout the day is:
_____
_____
_____

Successes, progress, or things I learned today: _____
_____
_____

**A negative emotion I battled today was:** _____

1. Was it appropriate to the situation*?  Yes ☐  No ☐
   (*Consider whether it was a real issue or influenced by mood, circumstance, or prior events.)
   - **If NO**, spend time in prayer and let it go, continually laying it at the feet of Jesus.
   - **If YES**, ask:
2. Is there anything productive* I can do about it?  Yes ☐  No ☐
   (*Consider whether it has potential to repair the issue & whether I will look back on the action with regret.)
   - **If NO**, spend time in prayer and let it go, continually laying it at the feet of Jesus.
   - **If YES**, ask:
3. What can I do, and how can I do it ASAP or implement a long-term plan? _____
   _____
   _____

4. Spend time in prayer and let it go, continually laying it at the feet of Jesus.

My prayer for the day: _____
_____
_____
_____

Random things I'd like to talk about, process, or remember: _____
_____
_____
_____

Today I'm thankful for: _____
_____
_____

**Anything about today that was:**
True: _____
Honorable: _____
Pure: _____
Lovely: _____
Admirable: _____
Excellent: _____
Worthy of Praise: _____

A negative thought/lie I'm trying to retrain is: _____
_____
_____
_____

A Bible verse to teach myself the truth when that thought/lie arises is:
_____
_____
_____

A song, Bible verse, or quote I'm going to ponder throughout the day is:
_____
_____
_____

Successes, progress, or things I learned today: _____
_____
_____

A negative emotion I battled today was: _____

1. Was it appropriate to the situation*?   Yes ☐  No ☐
   (*Consider whether it was a real issue or influenced by mood, circumstance, or prior events.)
   - **If NO**, spend time in prayer and let it go, continually laying it at the feet of Jesus.
   - **If YES**, ask:
2. Is there anything productive* I can do about it?   Yes ☐  No ☐
   (*Consider whether it has potential to repair the issue & whether I will look back on the action with regret.)
   - **If NO**, spend time in prayer and let it go, continually laying it at the feet of Jesus.
   - **If YES**, ask:
3. What can I do, and how can I do it ASAP or implement a long-term plan? _____
   _____
   _____

4. Spend time in prayer and let it go, continually laying it at the feet of Jesus.

My prayer for the day: _____
_____
_____
_____

Random things I'd like to talk about, process, or remember: _____
_____
_____
_____

**Today I'm thankful for:** _____
_____
_____

**Anything about today that was:**
True: _____
Honorable: _____
Pure: _____
Lovely: _____
Admirable: _____
Excellent: _____
Worthy of Praise: _____

**A negative thought/lie I'm trying to retrain is:** _____
_____
_____
_____

**A Bible verse to teach myself the truth when that thought/lie arises is:**
_____
_____
_____

**A song, Bible verse, or quote I'm going to ponder throughout the day is:**
_____
_____
_____

**Successes, progress, or things I learned today:** _____
_____
_____

**A negative emotion I battled today was:** _____

1. **Was it appropriate to the situation*?**   Yes ☐  No ☐
   (*Consider whether it was a real issue or influenced by mood, circumstance, or prior events.)
   - **If NO,** spend time in prayer and let it go, continually laying it at the feet of Jesus.
   - **If YES,** ask:
2. **Is there anything productive* I can do about it?**   Yes ☐  No ☐
   (*Consider whether it has potential to repair the issue & whether I will look back on the action with regret.)
   - **If NO,** spend time in prayer and let it go, continually laying it at the feet of Jesus.
   - **If YES,** ask:
3. **What can I do, and how can I do it ASAP or implement a long-term plan?** _____
   _____
   _____

4. **Spend time in prayer and let it go, continually laying it at the feet of Jesus.**

**My prayer for the day:** _____
_____
_____
_____

**Random things I'd like to talk about, process, or remember:** _____
_____
_____
_____

## Notes

# Exposing the Roots

Now let's talk more about digging into those root causes I mentioned earlier—roots that can drive some of our reactions and negative emotions subconsciously.

That's why I've included reflecting on prior experiences and thought patterns in the negative emotions section of the daily journaling.

Our feelings aren't always just reactions to what's currently happening; sometimes they're prompted by unhealed hurts from old wounds. This is especially noticeable in our *over*-reactions.

For example, I've snapped at my husband before in reaction to comments that really didn't deserve that kind of response. I've worked to become more intentional about analyzing those times, and I often find that he's poked a tender, unhealed wound—usually one he's completely unaware of.

In one instance, someone in my past had made me feel insecure, unworthy, stupid, and guilty for something that wasn't actually my fault, and what my husband said took me back there emotionally, though his comment was perfectly innocent.

This is an important thing to consider, because if we're not aware of it, we'll simply continue lashing out at people in ways that aren't appropriate to the situation, leaving them confused and hurt as well.

And even if someone has done something upsetting, we may react disproportionately because our emotions are heightened by something similar from our past. This all makes us more likely to respond aggressively rather than express our hurt in a productive way.

We also see what we expect to see. If someone in our past frequently made us feel neglected or rejected, then we'll be likely to see neglect and rejection where there is none or to see it as larger and more all-encompassing than it is.

For instance, let's pretend someone important to us once disappeared from our lives shortly after they started canceling plans and saying no to invitations. We may spiral into self-doubt or panic thinking that someone doesn't like us every time they say no or cancel plans now even if they have legitimate reasons and all other evidence tells us they genuinely enjoy our company.

You get the idea. The question is how to move forward from here.

Being aware of the issue is a great starting point. It can remind us to communicate in ways that facilitate solutions and to stay calm in the moment until we've had time to process our feelings.

It can still be quite difficult to trace feelings to their root issues, and, even when we do, knowing where those feelings came from—though important—doesn't solve the problem.

Those old hurts need healing, and digging into them often requires facing very painful memories—memories we may be intentionally avoiding.

While I have neither the space nor the qualifications to plumb this topic to its depths, I will share a few things that have helped me.

I've found journaling to be extremely valuable. It helps me expose all the pain I've been hiding from.

Sometimes I write a stream of consciousness account of the events and the way they made me feel. Sometimes I write in short story form using characters who experienced and felt the things I felt, even if the events might not exactly correlate. Sometimes I write as if I'm writing a memoir others will read.

With my most painful memories, this has been a process. The first time I write about them, they come out ugly—full of all the bitterness, anger, and whatever else I've been holding on to. If yours do too, that's okay. It's kind of the point. We can't work through our feelings if we won't be honest about them. I think we avoid this not only because we want to avoid thinking about the hurt, but because we don't like to face the ugliness it brings out in us.

Once I write it all out, I spend time in prayer. I ask God to meet me in that hurt, to remind me that He loves me, to show me that He was with me all along and grieves this hurt with me, and to reveal the lies this wound has embedded in my heart, whatever they might be, so that I can begin to replace them with the truth.

Then I do it all again—but not usually right that second. I may spend some days (or sometimes weeks) sitting with the Lord in that grief, repeating that prayer and whatever else feels like it needs to be discussed with Him.

When I write about the hurt a second time, it almost always comes out softer, less angry, and less ugly. I've purged some of the infection… but, usually, not all of it. So, I sit with the Lord some more, praying and asking Him to help me heal.

I do this however many times it takes before what I write and how I feel has God's fingerprint and grace all over it.

Eventually, my prayers must include both forgiveness and repentance. Without these, I will never be completely healed; the wound and the offender both still have power over me, my feelings, and my reactions.

I know forgiveness is hard, but we remember that when we forgive, we aren't saying the person is innocent. They wouldn't need forgiveness if they were. We're simply acknowledging that the forgiveness we received in Christ requires that we extend that same forgiveness to others (Matthew 18:21-35). If we can't forgive, somewhere deep down, we believe we deserve forgiveness, but that person does not. We don't truly understand what Christ has done for us even when we did not deserve it (Romans 5:8).

It's also helpful to remember that forgiveness isn't sweeping something under the rug and pretending it never happened, nor is it giving the person a free pass. There are relational consequences to wounds, and forgiveness doesn't mean we have to continue exposing ourselves to abuse.

And if you're worried about the offender "getting away with it," I recommend reading Psalm 37 and Psalm 73—repeatedly. These chapters remind us that we're not to be worried or upset by evildoers even when they seem to be thriving.

Here's a little snippet: "Better is the little of the righteous than the abundance of many wicked. For the arms of the wicked will be broken, but the Lord sustains the righteous. The Lord knows the days of the blameless, and their inheritance will be forever. They will not be ashamed in the time of evil, and in the days of famine they will have plenty. But the wicked will perish; and the enemies of the Lord will be like the glory of the pastures, they vanish—like smoke they vanish away" (Psalm 37:16-20).

But while justice is good and right, we also need to be careful that we don't rejoice when anyone suffers—even the wicked. Proverbs 24:17-18 says, "Do not rejoice when your enemy falls, and do not let your heart rejoice when he stumbles, otherwise, the Lord will see and be displeased and turn His anger away from him."

God is aware, and if He seems slow to judge, it's only because He's giving them the same chance to repent that we have had. In the end, unrepented injustice will not go unpunished (2 Peter 3:9). Our attitude is always that we should love and pray for our enemies to have that chance just as we did (Matthew 5:44-48). We're even to encourage other believers not to repay their enemies in kind. "See that no one repays another with evil for evil, but always seek what is good for one another and for all people" (1 Thessalonians 5:15).

It can feel impossible to even consider forgiving some atrocities, so it's also good to remember that forgiveness is a choice, not a feeling—just like love. It's an action we can do even when we don't feel like it. I recommend beginning by praying for them; it becomes increasingly difficult to despise or wish harm on someone when you're actively praying they'll receive the same unearned grace and forgiveness of Christ you've been given.

The world tells us that our actions should follow our feelings, but it leaves out the fact that our feelings actually follow our actions and our will. As we teach ourselves what to do, what to desire, and what to think, our feelings will align. As we choose to forgive, we will eventually find that we truly begin to feel forgiving.

I hear the objection that this isn't true forgiveness, but this isn't "fake it till you make it" any more than a beginner bench pressing ten pounds is fake lifting while they try to learn proper form and find out what they're capable of. It's not fake; it's training. Eventually, we'll be able to do the heavy lifting of forgiving from the heart.

As I work to forgive others, the Lord changes my feelings toward them. Thinking of the hurtful situation begins to lose its power to excite the same anger, bitterness, hurt, sorrow, or fear that it did before. It still doesn't feel good (it shouldn't), but I no longer feel captive to the power it held over me.

I begin to see that person as the Lord sees them—as worthy of love while they were yet sinners (Romans 5:8). And as I begin to see them through eyes of undeserved love instead of through the lens of my pain, I'm grieved at the spiteful way I had viewed them before. I truly do begin to seek their good (1 Thessalonians 5:15), and it sorrows me that I wasn't seeing them as the children of God He made them to be.

This is where we arrive at repentance. I know it may seem harsh in this context. Aren't we talking about ways others have wounded us?

But in addition to forgiving them, we also need to repent of the sinful ways we've reacted to them hurting us.

If someone hurt me, and I responded with bitterness, unforgiveness, angry outbursts, gossip, withholding God's love, or if I let that hurt ripple out into other relationships and hurt others, I'm still responsible for those actions, and I need to repent of them.

We can go back to Psalm 37 to see why: "Rest in the Lord and wait patiently for Him; do not get upset because of one who is successful in his way, because of the person who carries out wicked schemes. **Cease from anger and abandon wrath; do not get upset; it leads only to evildoing**" (Psalm 37:7-8, emphasis added).

God says that being angry, wrathful, and upset—even when it's because of the schemes of wicked people—leads only to evildoing.

Holding on to painful things in anger and bitterness gives the devil

## Taking Every Thought Captive

a foothold and causes trouble (Ephesians 4:26-27, Hebrews 12:15). Repentance is the second step toward gaining freedom over those events and aligning our reactions to God's will.

I don't want to oversimplify this. I know there are complicated situations—PTSD and nervous system overload, etc.—in which overcoming our reactions is not easy. It takes time and, often, professional help. But it's still our job to take ownership of that process, seek help, and work to conquer our sinful reactions with whatever resources we have.

Uncovering and addressing the roots of our negative emotions is a challenging but transformative journey. Though the process may be uncomfortable and even painful at times, it ultimately leads to freedom—freedom from the power of past hurts over our present lives, and freedom to respond with grace and confidence rather than react in anger or fear. Healing doesn't happen overnight, but as we partner with God in this work, we're not only transformed but also empowered to live with greater love, wisdom, and peace.

"THE WORLD TELLS US THAT OUR ACTIONS SHOULD FOLLOW OUR FEELINGS, BUT IT LEAVES OUT THE FACT THAT OUR FEELINGS ACTUALLY FOLLOW OUR ACTIONS AND OUR WILL."

Today I'm thankful for: _____
_____
_____

**Anything about today that was:**
True: _____
Honorable: _____
Pure: _____
Lovely: _____
Admirable: _____
Excellent: _____
Worthy of Praise: _____

A negative thought/lie I'm trying to retrain is: _____
_____
_____
_____

A Bible verse to teach myself the truth when that thought/lie arises is:
_____
_____
_____

A song, Bible verse, or quote I'm going to ponder throughout the day is:
_____
_____
_____

Successes, progress, or things I learned today: _____
_____
_____

A negative emotion I battled today was: _____

1. Was it appropriate to the situation*?   Yes ☐ No ☐
   (*Consider whether it was a real issue or influenced by mood, circumstance, or prior events.)
   - **If NO**, spend time in prayer and let it go, continually laying it at the feet of Jesus.
   - **If YES**, ask:
2. Is there anything productive* I can do about it?   Yes ☐ No ☐
   (*Consider whether it has potential to repair the issue & whether I will look back on the action with regret.)
   - **If NO**, spend time in prayer and let it go, continually laying it at the feet of Jesus.
   - **If YES**, ask:
3. What can I do, and how can I do it ASAP or implement a long-term plan?_____
   _____
   _____

4. Spend time in prayer and let it go, continually laying it at the feet of Jesus.

My prayer for the day: _____
_____
_____
_____

Random things I'd like to talk about, process, or remember: _____
_____
_____

**Today I'm thankful for:**


**Anything about today that was:**
True:
Honorable:
Pure:
Lovely:
Admirable:
Excellent:
Worthy of Praise:

**A negative thought/lie I'm trying to retrain is:**



**A Bible verse to teach myself the truth when that thought/lie arises is:**



**A song, Bible verse, or quote I'm going to ponder throughout the day is:**



**Successes, progress, or things I learned today:**

A negative emotion I battled today was: _____

1. Was it appropriate to the situation*?   Yes ☐  No ☐
   (*Consider whether it was a real issue or influenced by mood, circumstance, or prior events.)
   - **If NO**, spend time in prayer and let it go, continually laying it at the feet of Jesus.
   - **If YES**, ask:
2. Is there anything productive* I can do about it?   Yes ☐  No ☐
   (*Consider whether it has potential to repair the issue & whether I will look back on the action with regret.)
   - **If NO**, spend time in prayer and let it go, continually laying it at the feet of Jesus.
   - **If YES**, ask:
3. What can I do, and how can I do it ASAP or implement a long-term plan? _____
   _____
   _____

4. Spend time in prayer and let it go, continually laying it at the feet of Jesus.

My prayer for the day: _____
_____
_____

Random things I'd like to talk about, process, or remember: _____
_____
_____

Today I'm thankful for: _____
_____

**Anything about today that was:**
True: _____
Honorable: _____
Pure: _____
Lovely: _____
Admirable: _____
Excellent: _____
Worthy of Praise: _____

A negative thought/lie I'm trying to retrain is: _____
_____
_____
_____

A Bible verse to teach myself the truth when that thought/lie arises is:
_____
_____
_____

A song, Bible verse, or quote I'm going to ponder throughout the day is:
_____
_____
_____

Successes, progress, or things I learned today: _____
_____
_____

A negative emotion I battled today was: _____

1. Was it appropriate to the situation*?   Yes ☐  No ☐
   (*Consider whether it was a real issue or influenced by mood, circumstance, or prior events.)
   - **If NO**, spend time in prayer and let it go, continually laying it at the feet of Jesus.
   - **If YES**, ask:
2. Is there anything productive* I can do about it?   Yes ☐  No ☐
   (*Consider whether it has potential to repair the issue & whether I will look back on the action with regret.)
   - **If NO**, spend time in prayer and let it go, continually laying it at the feet of Jesus.
   - **If YES**, ask:
3. What can I do, and how can I do it ASAP or implement a long-term plan? _____
   _____
   _____

4. Spend time in prayer and let it go, continually laying it at the feet of Jesus.

My prayer for the day: _____
_____
_____
_____

Random things I'd like to talk about, process, or remember: _____
_____
_____
_____

Today I'm thankful for: _____
_____
_____

Anything about today that was:
True: _____
Honorable: _____
Pure: _____
Lovely: _____
Admirable: _____
Excellent: _____
Worthy of Praise: _____

A negative thought/lie I'm trying to retrain is: _____
_____
_____
_____

A Bible verse to teach myself the truth when that thought/lie arises is:
_____
_____
_____

A song, Bible verse, or quote I'm going to ponder throughout the day is:
_____
_____
_____

Successes, progress, or things I learned today: _____
_____
_____

A negative emotion I battled today was: _____

1. Was it appropriate to the situation*?    Yes ☐  No ☐
   (*Consider whether it was a real issue or influenced by mood, circumstance, or prior events.)
   - **If NO**, spend time in prayer and let it go, continually laying it at the feet of Jesus.
   - **If YES**, ask:
2. Is there anything productive* I can do about it?    Yes ☐  No ☐
   (*Consider whether it has potential to repair the issue & whether I will look back on the action with regret.)
   - **If NO**, spend time in prayer and let it go, continually laying it at the feet of Jesus.
   - **If YES**, ask:
3. What can I do, and how can I do it ASAP or implement a long-term plan? _____
   _____
   _____

4. Spend time in prayer and let it go, continually laying it at the feet of Jesus.

My prayer for the day: _____
_____
_____
_____

Random things I'd like to talk about, process, or remember: _____
_____
_____

107

Today I'm thankful for: _____
_____
_____

**Anything about today that was:**
True: _____
Honorable: _____
Pure: _____
Lovely: _____
Admirable: _____
Excellent: _____
Worthy of Praise: _____

**A negative thought/lie I'm trying to retrain is:** _____
_____
_____
_____

**A Bible verse to teach myself the truth when that thought/lie arises is:**
_____
_____
_____

**A song, Bible verse, or quote I'm going to ponder throughout the day is:**
_____
_____
_____

**Successes, progress, or things I learned today:** _____
_____
_____

**A negative emotion I battled today was:** _____

1. **Was it appropriate to the situation*?**  Yes ☐  No ☐
   (*Consider whether it was a real issue or influenced by mood, circumstance, or prior events.)
   - **If NO**, spend time in prayer and let it go, continually laying it at the feet of Jesus.
   - **If YES**, ask:

2. **Is there anything productive* I can do about it?**  Yes ☐  No ☐
   (*Consider whether it has potential to repair the issue & whether I will look back on the action with regret.)
   - **If NO**, spend time in prayer and let it go, continually laying it at the feet of Jesus.
   - **If YES**, ask:

3. What can I do, and how can I do it ASAP or implement a long-term plan? _____
   _____
   _____

4. Spend time in prayer and let it go, continually laying it at the feet of Jesus.

**My prayer for the day:** _____
_____
_____
_____

**Random things I'd like to talk about, process, or remember:** _____
_____
_____
_____

Today I'm thankful for: _____
_____
_____

**Anything about today that was:**
True: _____
Honorable: _____
Pure: _____
Lovely: _____
Admirable: _____
Excellent: _____
Worthy of Praise: _____

A negative thought/lie I'm trying to retrain is: _____
_____
_____
_____

A Bible verse to teach myself the truth when that thought/lie arises is:
_____
_____
_____

A song, Bible verse, or quote I'm going to ponder throughout the day is:
_____
_____
_____

Successes, progress, or things I learned today: _____
_____
_____

**A negative emotion I battled today was:** ───────────

1. Was it appropriate to the situation*?  Yes ☐  No ☐
   (*Consider whether it was a real issue or influenced by mood, circumstance, or prior events.)
   - **If NO**, spend time in prayer and let it go, continually laying it at the feet of Jesus.
   - **If YES**, ask:
2. Is there anything productive* I can do about it?  Yes ☐  No ☐
   (*Consider whether it has potential to repair the issue & whether I will look back on the action with regret.)
   - **If NO**, spend time in prayer and let it go, continually laying it at the feet of Jesus.
   - **If YES**, ask:
3. What can I do, and how can I do it ASAP or implement a long-term plan? ─────────────
   ─────────────────────────
   ─────────────────────────

4. Spend time in prayer and let it go, continually laying it at the feet of Jesus.

My prayer for the day: ─────────────────
─────────────────────────
─────────────────────────
─────────────────────────

Random things I'd like to talk about, process, or remember: ────
─────────────────────────
─────────────────────────

Today I'm thankful for: _____
_____
_____

**Anything about today that was:**
True: _____
Honorable: _____
Pure: _____
Lovely: _____
Admirable: _____
Excellent: _____
Worthy of Praise: _____

A negative thought/lie I'm trying to retrain is: _____
_____
_____
_____

A Bible verse to teach myself the truth when that thought/lie arises is:
_____
_____
_____

A song, Bible verse, or quote I'm going to ponder throughout the day is:
_____
_____
_____

Successes, progress, or things I learned today: _____
_____
_____

A negative emotion I battled today was: _____

1. Was it appropriate to the situation*?   Yes ☐  No ☐
   (*Consider whether it was a real issue or influenced by mood, circumstance, or prior events.)
   - **If NO**, spend time in prayer and let it go, continually laying it at the feet of Jesus.
   - **If YES**, ask:
2. Is there anything productive* I can do about it?   Yes ☐  No ☐
   (*Consider whether it has potential to repair the issue & whether I will look back on the action with regret.)
   - **If NO**, spend time in prayer and let it go, continually laying it at the feet of Jesus.
   - **If YES**, ask:
3. What can I do, and how can I do it ASAP or implement a long-term plan? _____
   _____
   _____

4. Spend time in prayer and let it go, continually laying it at the feet of Jesus.

My prayer for the day: _____
_____
_____
_____

Random things I'd like to talk about, process, or remember: _____
_____
_____
_____

**Notes**

# Spiritual Motion Sickness

Another way to cultivate peace in our hearts and minds is to live out the things we truly believe and value.

When I started paying attention to my mood, I noticed that sometimes it declined as the day went on, leaving me a grumpy mess by the time evening rolled around.

Eventually, I recognized the pattern: the less I did what I believed I should be doing and what I said I thought was important, the worse I felt about myself, and therefore about my day.

In the morning, I could see all the possibilities. But as the chance to do meaningful and useful things slipped away, I became annoyed and regretful that I'd wasted it. I became more and more disillusioned by my failure to live up to the day's potential.

We have an image of our ideal self, and when we're not working to achieve it, we're violating our core values. It feels like we're betraying ourselves.

This can sound like I mean we all need to accomplish *more*—a thing that usually feels impossible and overwhelming—but it often just means we need to accomplish something *different*.

Many of us truly need to do *less* in our lives, but we may need to do more *of value*—things that align with our beliefs and priorities. This will often require examining what those beliefs and priorities are.

We'll come back to both ideas in the next section.

For now, we'll focus on those of us who pretty much know what we should be doing; we just aren't doing it consistently, and we're filled with dissatisfaction.

## Taking Every Thought Captive

I call this "spiritual motion sickness."

Motion sickness is explained like this: "Our brains sense movement by getting signals from our inner ears, eyes, muscles, and joints. When they get signals that don't match, we can get motion sickness."

In the same way, when our minds and hearts say one thing, but our actions aren't following, the discrepancy shows up as unease, irritability, and low self-image—a sort of spiritual nausea that might be expressed as anything from anger to depression.

Our peace will only be restored when we begin working to become the person we know we should be. We'll never *finish* becoming that person, but as long as we're working diligently toward it, we can resolve the current problem of our actions and thoughts not matching our beliefs and values.

It's easy to dive into this with an all-or-nothing mindset that will leave us overwhelmed and failing. If we jump in trying to change everything about ourselves instantly, we'll almost always give up.

Becoming our ideal self (which is also the person God created us to be) is a lifelong process that requires wading slowly ever deeper into one choice after another.

To get started, ask yourself, "What is one area of my life I'm dissatisfied with that I have the power to change?"

Pick one that eats at the back of your mind and doesn't let you rest or relax.

And I included that bit about it being something you have the power to change for a reason. A goal like "Hit the New York Times best seller list" comes with many factors we have no control over. However, something like "Write the best book I'm capable of writing" is thoroughly within our power.

Someone once told me their long-term goal was to get married within a certain number of years. While that may be a desire, it isn't a goal, because it can't be accomplished unless 1) you find someone you want to marry and 2) they also want to marry you. These are not things we can guarantee through our own determination. A good goal for that person might be "I'm going to work to get out and meet more people and grow as a person so that if a potential spouse comes along, I'll be in a good place for that relationship." This goal has the wonderful side effects of helping to create a more supportive community through meeting more people and building a stronger, more positive, and more contented internal life through personal growth—things that benefit that person whether they ever marry or not.

A muddier differentiation can be found in the following example: "Reconcile with my estranged mother" vs. "Work toward reconciling with my estranged mother." The reconciliation isn't guaranteed, because your mother might not be on board, but working toward reconciliation is something you can do regardless of their response (Romans 12:18).

The goal can't be something dependent on other people or on the world's response; it must be something achievable through your own effort, given enough time and perseverance.

So maybe it's a cluttered house, a weight problem, overindulgence in shopping, a broken relationship, poor time management, a sin you've never gotten victory over, or neglecting some work God's called you to.

Start there and create goals to that end. Working toward these goals means we can answer, "Yes!" when we ask ourselves, "Am I actively working to become the person I want to be and the person God made me to be?"

When I can speak that yes, I physically feel the stress in my body dissipate. Though I must acknowledge that it will take many small steps, I know I'm on the way, and the journey will be worth it.

There are several books I recommend to help with this. None of them are books of faith, so while I can't whole-heartedly endorse everything in them and I feel the essential spiritual component is missing, they all have valuable insights.

The first is *The Happiness Advantage* by Shawn Achor. This book focuses on why it's in our best interest to look at life positively. Many of us think our mindset is fixed and we're doomed to continue on as we always have. *The Happiness Advantage* not only reminds us that change is possible, it gives tips on how to develop that forward motion.

Achor discusses how lowering the barrier to simply *starting* a task we've typically found difficult can push us in the right direction. Beginning is often the hardest part.

If we also increase the difficulty of whatever task we've usually done in its place, we gain even more momentum.

He uses the example that he'd always wanted to learn to play the guitar, but day after day, he found himself coming home and turning on the TV instead. His guitar was in the closet—out of sight, out of mind. Finally, he pulled it into the middle of the floor.

He found that turning on the TV was still too easy, so he also removed the batteries from his remote. With the ease of the guitar sitting right in front of him plus the extra barrier interfering with his TV watching, he finally started learning to play. These two steps combined to give him the prod he needed to override an ingrained habit.

Of course, he knew where the batteries were and could've put them back in the remote at any moment, but the extra steps required would've solidified that it was a *choice* to watch TV rather than practice and would've further disillusioned him about who he was vs. who he wanted to be.

So once you've identified the area in which you have the most spiritual motion sickness, look for ways to make the steps toward that goal easier while making the current actions that get in the way more difficult.

If it's healthy eating, spend some time meal planning and discovering healthy snacks that aren't a lot of trouble, but also remove the food you don't want to eat from your house. If this isn't possible due to other family members not being on board, perhaps get a small safe for snack foods they want on hand, and make sure you don't know the code.

Another tip that helped me came from the book *Stolen Focus* by Johann Hari. He talks about feeling "diminished" when not working toward his goals or when actively choosing tasks that don't align with his values. This was a good measure for me. It's how I feel when I'm getting further away from the person I want to be rather than closer to it.

For instance, scrolling my social media app of choice for fifteen minutes may feel all right, but if I continue mindlessly watching inane reels with no limits, I soon find myself feeling diminished. As my time on

## Spiritual Motion Sickness

social media increases, my level of self-worth decreases. I could say the same about eating one brownie vs. three.

There are also activities that make us feel diminished immediately; any overt sin will do so. Most of us know what those things are.

I hope I'm not alone in having a distinct answer when I ask myself if I'm feeling diminished or not. If you're unsure, ask yourself what your future self will be happiest with. At 6 P.M. when you feel like vegging in front of the TV, ask yourself if your 10 P.M. self will be glad or annoyed with that decision. If you can see that you'd be frustrated by your choice later, it's time to switch gears.

It's important to note that if we already feel diminished by poor choices, we don't have to carry that momentum into the rest of the day. We can shift now and start working toward our goals instead of away from them. When I do so, that restless, grouchy, couch-potato feeling begins to subside, and I gain a sense of control over my day and myself. Ending the day on a good note creates a feeling of accomplishment that's more likely to snowball into the next day and keep me motivated to work toward my goals.

The last book I'll mention is *The War of Art* by Steven Pressfield. This book discusses something Pressfield calls "resistance"—the feeling that something always opposes our efforts to do better. "Resistance," he says, "only opposes in one direction. [It] obstructs movement only from a lower sphere to a higher. It kicks in when we seek to pursue a calling in the arts, launch an innovative enterprise, or evolve to a higher station morally, ethically, or spiritually."

As believers, we know this resistance is multifaceted; it involves both our flesh's immediate desires and the devil's temptation. This discomfort can only be overcome by putting in the discipline it takes to push past it and begin living our values.

And despite messages to the contrary, we're not actually the happiest or most fulfilled when we indulge our every whim. Happiness and fulfillment come when we're working toward the things we value and know are important.

Working toward those things might be counter to our immediate de-

## Taking Every Thought Captive

sires—flesh vs. spirit, as the Bible puts it. "For the flesh desires what is contrary to the Spirit, and the Spirit what is contrary to the flesh. They are in conflict with each other, so that you are not to do whatever you want" (Galatians 5:17).

Choosing "not to do whatever you want" isn't automatic. It's a process, but self-control is a key component in having positive feelings about ourselves and our lives.

We'll never be perfect, but we can make consistent, intentional progress toward becoming the person we were created to be. It takes discipline, reflection, forethought, and sometimes creative strategies to overcome resistance—whether from our flesh, habits, or external temptations.

By beginning this journey, we can gradually close the gap between who we are and who we want to be, easing the "spiritual motion sickness" that comes from living out of sync with our core values. The work is difficult and never finished, but the rewards—contentment, fulfillment, purpose, self-respect, and a closer walk with God—are well worth the effort.

"We have an image of our ideal self, and when we're not working to achieve it, we're violating our core values. It feels like we're betraying ourselves."

Today I'm thankful for: _____
_____
_____

**Anything about today that was:**
True: _____
Honorable: _____
Pure: _____
Lovely: _____
Admirable: _____
Excellent: _____
Worthy of Praise: _____

A negative thought/lie I'm trying to retrain is: ____
_____
_____
_____

A Bible verse to teach myself the truth when that thought/lie arises is:
_____
_____
_____

A song, Bible verse, or quote I'm going to ponder throughout the day is:
_____
_____
_____

Successes, progress, or things I learned today: _____
_____
_____

**A negative emotion I battled today was:** _____

1. Was it appropriate to the situation*?    Yes ☐  No ☐
   (*Consider whether it was a real issue or influenced by mood, circumstance, or prior events.)
   - **If NO,** spend time in prayer and let it go, continually laying it at the feet of Jesus.
   - **If YES,** ask:
2. Is there anything productive* I can do about it?  Yes ☐  No ☐
   (*Consider whether it has potential to repair the issue & whether I will look back on the action with regret.)
   - **If NO,** spend time in prayer and let it go, continually laying it at the feet of Jesus.
   - **If YES,** ask:
3. What can I do, and how can I do it ASAP or implement a long-term plan? _____
   _____
   _____

4. Spend time in prayer and let it go, continually laying it at the feet of Jesus.

**My prayer for the day:** _____
_____
_____
_____

**Random things I'd like to talk about, process, or remember:** _____
_____
_____

Today I'm thankful for: _____
_____
_____

**Anything about today that was:**
True: _____
Honorable: _____
Pure: _____
Lovely: _____
Admirable: _____
Excellent: _____
Worthy of Praise: _____

A negative thought/lie I'm trying to retrain is: _____
_____
_____
_____

A Bible verse to teach myself the truth when that thought/lie arises is:
_____
_____
_____

A song, Bible verse, or quote I'm going to ponder throughout the day is:
_____
_____
_____

Successes, progress, or things I learned today: _____
_____
_____

A negative emotion I battled today was: _____

1. Was it appropriate to the situation*?  Yes ☐  No ☐
   (*Consider whether it was a real issue or influenced by mood, circumstance, or prior events.)
   - If **NO**, spend time in prayer and let it go, continually laying it at the feet of Jesus.
   - If **YES**, ask:
2. Is there anything productive* I can do about it?  Yes ☐  No ☐
   (*Consider whether it has potential to repair the issue & whether I will look back on the action with regret.)
   - If **NO**, spend time in prayer and let it go, continually laying it at the feet of Jesus.
   - If **YES**, ask:
3. What can I do, and how can I do it ASAP or implement a long-term plan? _____
   _____
   _____

4. Spend time in prayer and let it go, continually laying it at the feet of Jesus.

My prayer for the day: _____
_____
_____
_____

Random things I'd like to talk about, process, or remember: _____
_____
_____

Today I'm thankful for: _____
_____
_____

**Anything about today that was:**
True: _____
Honorable: _____
Pure: _____
Lovely: _____
Admirable: _____
Excellent: _____
Worthy of Praise: _____

A negative thought/lie I'm trying to retrain is: _____
_____
_____
_____

A Bible verse to teach myself the truth when that thought/lie arises is:
_____
_____
_____

A song, Bible verse, or quote I'm going to ponder throughout the day is:
_____
_____
_____

Successes, progress, or things I learned today: _____
_____
_____

A negative emotion I battled today was: _____

1. Was it appropriate to the situation*?  Yes ☐  No ☐
   (*Consider whether it was a real issue or influenced by mood, circumstance, or prior events.)
   - **If NO**, spend time in prayer and let it go, continually laying it at the feet of Jesus.
   - **If YES**, ask:
2. Is there anything productive* I can do about it?  Yes ☐  No ☐
   (*Consider whether it has potential to repair the issue & whether I will look back on the action with regret.)
   - **If NO**, spend time in prayer and let it go, continually laying it at the feet of Jesus.
   - **If YES**, ask:
3. What can I do, and how can I do it ASAP or implement a long-term plan? _____
   _____
   _____

4. Spend time in prayer and let it go, continually laying it at the feet of Jesus.

My prayer for the day: _____
_____
_____
_____

Random things I'd like to talk about, process, or remember: _____
_____
_____

Today I'm thankful for: _____
_____
_____

**Anything about today that was:**
True: _____
Honorable: _____
Pure: _____
Lovely: _____
Admirable: _____
Excellent: _____
Worthy of Praise: _____

A negative thought/lie I'm trying to retrain is: _____
_____
_____
_____

A Bible verse to teach myself the truth when that thought/lie arises is:
_____
_____
_____

A song, Bible verse, or quote I'm going to ponder throughout the day is:
_____
_____
_____

Successes, progress, or things I learned today: _____
_____
_____

A negative emotion I battled today was: _____

1. Was it appropriate to the situation*?   Yes ☐   No ☐
   (*Consider whether it was a real issue or influenced by mood, circumstance, or prior events.)
   - **If NO**, spend time in prayer and let it go, continually laying it at the feet of Jesus.
   - **If YES**, ask:
2. Is there anything productive* I can do about it?   Yes ☐   No ☐
   (*Consider whether it has potential to repair the issue & whether I will look back on the action with regret.)
   - **If NO**, spend time in prayer and let it go, continually laying it at the feet of Jesus.
   - **If YES**, ask:
3. What can I do, and how can I do it ASAP or implement a long-term plan? _____
   _____
   _____

4. Spend time in prayer and let it go, continually laying it at the feet of Jesus.

My prayer for the day: _____
_____
_____
_____

Random things I'd like to talk about, process, or remember: _____
_____
_____
_____

Today I'm thankful for: _____
_____
_____

**Anything about today that was:**
True: _____
Honorable: _____
Pure: _____
Lovely: _____
Admirable: _____
Excellent: _____
Worthy of Praise: _____

A negative thought/lie I'm trying to retrain is: _____
_____
_____
_____

A Bible verse to teach myself the truth when that thought/lie arises is:
_____
_____
_____

A song, Bible verse, or quote I'm going to ponder throughout the day is:
_____
_____
_____

Successes, progress, or things I learned today: _____
_____
_____

A negative emotion I battled today was: _____

1. Was it appropriate to the situation*?   Yes ☐   No ☐
   (*Consider whether it was a real issue or influenced by mood, circumstance, or prior events.)
   - **If NO**, spend time in prayer and let it go, continually laying it at the feet of Jesus.
   - **If YES**, ask:
2. Is there anything productive* I can do about it?   Yes ☐   No ☐
   (*Consider whether it has potential to repair the issue & whether I will look back on the action with regret.)
   - **If NO**, spend time in prayer and let it go, continually laying it at the feet of Jesus.
   - **If YES**, ask:
3. What can I do, and how can I do it ASAP or implement a long-term plan? _____
   _____
   _____

4. Spend time in prayer and let it go, continually laying it at the feet of Jesus.

My prayer for the day: _____
_____
_____
_____

Random things I'd like to talk about, process, or remember: _____
_____
_____

Today I'm thankful for: _____
_____
_____

Anything about today that was:
True: _____
Honorable: _____
Pure: _____
Lovely: _____
Admirable: _____
Excellent: _____
Worthy of Praise: _____

A negative thought/lie I'm trying to retrain is: _____
_____
_____
_____

A Bible verse to teach myself the truth when that thought/lie arises is:
_____
_____
_____

A song, Bible verse, or quote I'm going to ponder throughout the day is:
_____
_____
_____

Successes, progress, or things I learned today: _____
_____
_____

**A negative emotion I battled today was:** _____

1. **Was it appropriate to the situation*?**   Yes ☐  No ☐
   (*Consider whether it was a real issue or influenced by mood, circumstance, or prior events.)
   - **If NO**, spend time in prayer and let it go, continually laying it at the feet of Jesus.
   - **If YES**, ask:
2. **Is there anything productive* I can do about it?**   Yes ☐  No ☐
   (*Consider whether it has potential to repair the issue & whether I will look back on the action with regret.)
   - **If NO**, spend time in prayer and let it go, continually laying it at the feet of Jesus.
   - **If YES**, ask:
3. What can I do, and how can I do it ASAP or implement a long-term plan? _____
   _____
   _____

4. Spend time in prayer and let it go, continually laying it at the feet of Jesus.

**My prayer for the day:** _____
_____
_____
_____

**Random things I'd like to talk about, process, or remember:** _____
_____
_____
_____

Today I'm thankful for: _____
_____
_____

**Anything about today that was:**
True: _____
Honorable: _____
Pure: _____
Lovely: _____
Admirable: _____
Excellent: _____
Worthy of Praise: _____

A negative thought/lie I'm trying to retrain is: _____
_____
_____
_____

A Bible verse to teach myself the truth when that thought/lie arises is:
_____
_____
_____

A song, Bible verse, or quote I'm going to ponder throughout the day is:
_____
_____
_____

Successes, progress, or things I learned today: _____
_____
_____

**A negative emotion I battled today was:** _____

1. Was it appropriate to the situation*?  Yes ☐  No ☐
   (*Consider whether it was a real issue or influenced by mood, circumstance, or prior events.)
   - **If NO**, spend time in prayer and let it go, continually laying it at the feet of Jesus.
   - **If YES**, ask:
2. Is there anything productive* I can do about it?  Yes ☐  No ☐
   (*Consider whether it has potential to repair the issue & whether I will look back on the action with regret.)
   - **If NO**, spend time in prayer and let it go, continually laying it at the feet of Jesus.
   - **If YES**, ask:
3. What can I do, and how can I do it ASAP or implement a long-term plan?_____
   _____
   _____

4. Spend time in prayer and let it go, continually laying it at the feet of Jesus.

**My prayer for the day:** _____
_____
_____
_____

**Random things I'd like to talk about, process, or remember:** _____
_____
_____

**Notes**

# The Small Things

Another way to cultivate contentment in our lives is to see everything we do as planting a seed.

I recognize that this is not always easy to do. We want to see the fruit from what we've done today instantly. We don't want to wait.

But that's not how it works. Fruit grows over time as the continual hard work of planting, watering, pruning, pest-control, weeding, and fertilizing is done.

The farmer doesn't plant a seed and give up because he doesn't have an ear of corn the next morning. Nor does he stand beside his field wringing his hands, worrying whether it will ever amount to anything.

He plants the seed, does his work diligently, trusts the process, and trusts God. Day in and day out, he shows up and does the work.

For many of us, when we plant the seeds of a new beginning, all we see in front of us is a long season of uncertainty and hard work with no guarantees. We barely dare to hope that something beautiful and nourishing will grow from it, because all we can see are the obstacles and the potential for failure. Maybe we'll do it wrong. Maybe we can't do it at all. Maybe something outside of our control will wreck it. Maybe even if we do it perfectly, it won't yield what we expect. Maybe we'll do it all, and it won't really matter.

Many of us carry a seed around with us all the time. It's in our pocket, poking us every time we sit down—a little nagging thing we can't get rid of and can't ignore. We take it out every now and then to gaze at it longingly. Too many of us let all those thoughts of fear and doubt overwhelm us, and in the end, stuff the seed back in our pocket with a sigh of defeat and dejection.

## Taking Every Thought Captive

The fear of failure, emptiness, and purposelessness keeps us from moving forward. But here's the thing: by never taking the steps, *we guarantee the thing we fear.*

I had a conversation with a young man who had an idea for a business venture. It was completely within the scope of reality to pursue it; he had the time, the money, and the skills to begin. But when encouraged to move forward, he said, "I don't know; I just don't know if it will work."

But what this young man regularly did with that time instead was play video games. He was afraid that he would spend a lot of time doing something that wouldn't matter in the end, so instead, he spent a lot of time doing something that was *guaranteed* not to matter in the end. The time will pass either way.

I'm not vilifying video games. They're a fine hobby when you need to relax, just like working puzzles or reading a book, and they can be a meaningful way to spend quality time with others. But when any hobby takes an excessive amount of our time or becomes what we do instead of planting that seed, it's time to take a second look at the place it has in our lives.

So maybe ask yourself, "Is there something I want to do, but I'm not doing it because I'm scared?" If there is, take some time to write out the first few steps. Don't try to plan the whole thing, and don't try to learn everything you'll need for every step before you begin. Learn what you need for the first step, then the next, then the next. Plant the seed. Water it. Wait. Weed. Rejoice when you see the tiny shoot.

The Parable of the Talents reminds us that everything God has given us is given for the purpose of "investing" it in His work. He hasn't left any of us out, nor is He asking anything we're incapable of. Whatever we're given is based on our abilities. Taking that seed and putting it back in our pocket because we're afraid isn't a valid excuse, as we can read in this story (Matthew 25:14-30).

For me, I know the big tasks often seem insurmountable. If it's something I can't complete TODAY, it feels like I can't do it at all. Now, when I feel the "I can't do this" arising in the pit of my stomach, I change it to, "It's going to take time to do this, and that's okay."

# The Small Things

I will not despise the day of small things but rather rejoice as the Lord did when Zerubbabel simply held the plumb line in his hand to begin planning the rebuilding of the temple (Zechariah 4:10). I make it a point to rejoice over every tiny step on the road to accomplishing a goal rather than feel defeated because it isn't finished yet.

Elisabeth Elliot says in *Secure in the Everlasting Arms*, "Today is mine. Tomorrow is none of my business. If I peer anxiously into the fog of the future, I will strain my spiritual eyes so that I will not see clearly what is required of me now."

That's usually our trouble; we're attempting to focus too far into the future. "So do not worry about tomorrow; for tomorrow will worry about itself. Each day has enough trouble of its own" (Matthew 6:34).

We can't pre-water the crop for tomorrow. We can't prune the vines before they've grown big enough. Today is the only day we can truly focus on. I've strained my spiritual eyes in the past, trying to focus on all the many things I'd like to do at once—more book ideas alone than I could write in a lifetime. I used to get really anxious about the how and when and if....

One day while feeling this way, I was reading *Oswald Chambers: Abandoned to God* by David McCasland. Apparently, a piece of advice Chambers gave regularly was, "Trust God, and do the next thing."

That advice began popping up everywhere in my life over the next days and weeks. It became a catchphrase for me any time I was feeling overwhelmed or anxious about how, when, and whether my seeds were going to grow.

My job is simply to do the next thing—to be obedient to the Lord's direction and do the duties I can do in this moment. Sometimes those duties have nothing to do with cultivating that specific field.

Just as that farmer doesn't spend every day and hour watching his crop, we also have other tasks and relationships to attend to if we're going to love others well and live our lives with integrity.

And sometimes we don't even know what we're planting; we're just doing what life requires of us at that moment and caring for others. Joseph didn't know that asking two fellow inmates why they looked sad would result in his eventual release from prison and the salvation of nations from famine (Genesis 40:7). David didn't know that taking food to his brothers in battle would result in him defeating Goliath (1 Samuel 17:17-51). Ruth didn't know that committing to care for her mother-in-law and leaving her own people would result in her marrying again and becoming an ancestor of Jesus (Book of Ruth).

Had they set out with those outcomes as goals instead of setting out to love the people around them, they probably would have failed. When we're faithful in the small things, we prove that we will be faithful in much. When we're unrighteous in the little things, we prove that we will be unrighteous in much (Luke 16:10).

As we've talked about before, the main thing isn't to have huge earthly goals. By planting a seed, I don't mean it has to be the worldly idea of "chasing our dreams." I mean that we plant and tend whatever God has given us—small or big—faithfully. We trust him with the outcome. "Neither the one who plants nor the one who waters is anything, but God who causes the growth" (1 Corinthians 3:7).

In all scenarios, we can imagine God as the sun. The farmer can do all the work he wants, but if the sun doesn't shine, the crops won't grow. He has to trust the sun every year, day in and day out.

The same is true of us any time we plant something. The growth is never up to us. We can't make it happen if it isn't powered by our great God, but God uses the seeds we plant and tend to bring about the good fruit. We trust the growth to Him.

We don't have to be afraid to step out where faith calls, whether that be into a battle with a giant like David or leaving everything we know to care for a mother-in-law like Ruth.

The seed you need to plant may be small or large. It might be gaining the courage to start a new friendship, adopt a child, change jobs, write your book, or launch that business idea.

Whatever it is and wherever you are, you can, "Trust God, and do the next thing." You don't have to worry about the outcome. You plant and water. God causes the growth.

"The fear of failure, emptiness, and purposelessness keeps us from moving forward. But here's the thing: by never taking the steps, we guarantee the thing we fear."

Today I'm thankful for: _____
_____
_____

**Anything about today that was:**
True: _____
Honorable: _____
Pure: _____
Lovely: _____
Admirable: _____
Excellent: _____
Worthy of Praise: _____

A negative thought/lie I'm trying to retrain is: _____
_____
_____
_____

A Bible verse to teach myself the truth when that thought/lie arises is:
_____
_____
_____

A song, Bible verse, or quote I'm going to ponder throughout the day is:
_____
_____
_____

Successes, progress, or things I learned today: _____
_____
_____

A negative emotion I battled today was: _____

1. Was it appropriate to the situation*?    Yes ☐  No ☐
   (*Consider whether it was a real issue or influenced by mood, circumstance, or prior events.)
   - **If NO**, spend time in prayer and let it go, continually laying it at the feet of Jesus.
   - **If YES**, ask:
2. Is there anything productive* I can do about it?  Yes ☐  No ☐
   (*Consider whether it has potential to repair the issue & whether I will look back on the action with regret.)
   - **If NO**, spend time in prayer and let it go, continually laying it at the feet of Jesus.
   - **If YES**, ask:
3. What can I do, and how can I do it ASAP or implement a long-term plan? _____
   _____
   _____

4. Spend time in prayer and let it go, continually laying it at the feet of Jesus.

My prayer for the day: _____
_____
_____
_____

Random things I'd like to talk about, process, or remember: _____
_____
_____
_____

Today I'm thankful for: _____
_____
_____

Anything about today that was:
True: _____
Honorable: _____
Pure: _____
Lovely: _____
Admirable: _____
Excellent: _____
Worthy of Praise: _____

A negative thought/lie I'm trying to retrain is: _____
_____
_____
_____

A Bible verse to teach myself the truth when that thought/lie arises is:
_____
_____
_____

A song, Bible verse, or quote I'm going to ponder throughout the day is:
_____
_____
_____

Successes, progress, or things I learned today: _____
_____
_____

A negative emotion I battled today was: _____

1. Was it appropriate to the situation*?   Yes ☐  No ☐
   (*Consider whether it was a real issue or influenced by mood, circumstance, or prior events.)
   - **If NO**, spend time in prayer and let it go, continually laying it at the feet of Jesus.
   - **If YES**, ask:
2. Is there anything productive* I can do about it?   Yes ☐  No ☐
   (*Consider whether it has potential to repair the issue & whether I will look back on the action with regret.)
   - **If NO**, spend time in prayer and let it go, continually laying it at the feet of Jesus.
   - **If YES**, ask:
3. What can I do, and how can I do it ASAP or implement a long-term plan? _____
   _____
   _____

4. Spend time in prayer and let it go, continually laying it at the feet of Jesus.

My prayer for the day: _____
_____
_____
_____

Random things I'd like to talk about, process, or remember: _____
_____
_____
_____

Today I'm thankful for: _____
_____
_____

**Anything about today that was:**
True: _____
Honorable: _____
Pure: _____
Lovely: _____
Admirable: _____
Excellent: _____
Worthy of Praise: _____

A negative thought/lie I'm trying to retrain is: _____
_____
_____
_____

A Bible verse to teach myself the truth when that thought/lie arises is:
_____
_____
_____

A song, Bible verse, or quote I'm going to ponder throughout the day is:
_____
_____
_____

Successes, progress, or things I learned today: _____
_____
_____

**A negative emotion I battled today was:** _____

1. Was it appropriate to the situation*?  Yes ☐  No ☐
   (*Consider whether it was a real issue or influenced by mood, circumstance, or prior events.)
   - **If NO**, spend time in prayer and let it go, continually laying it at the feet of Jesus.
   - **If YES**, ask:
2. Is there anything productive* I can do about it?  Yes ☐  No ☐
   (*Consider whether it has potential to repair the issue & whether I will look back on the action with regret.)
   - **If NO**, spend time in prayer and let it go, continually laying it at the feet of Jesus.
   - **If YES**, ask:
3. What can I do, and how can I do it ASAP or implement a long-term plan?_____
   _____
   _____

4. Spend time in prayer and let it go, continually laying it at the feet of Jesus.

**My prayer for the day:** _____
_____
_____
_____

**Random things I'd like to talk about, process, or remember:** _____
_____
_____
_____

Today I'm thankful for: _____
_____
_____

**Anything about today that was:**
True: _____
Honorable: _____
Pure: _____
Lovely: _____
Admirable: _____
Excellent: _____
Worthy of Praise: _____

A negative thought/lie I'm trying to retrain is: _____
_____
_____
_____

A Bible verse to teach myself the truth when that thought/lie arises is:
_____
_____
_____

A song, Bible verse, or quote I'm going to ponder throughout the day is:
_____
_____
_____

Successes, progress, or things I learned today: _____
_____
_____

A negative emotion I battled today was: _____

1. Was it appropriate to the situation*?   Yes ☐  No ☐
   (*Consider whether it was a real issue or influenced by mood, circumstance, or prior events.)
   - **If NO**, spend time in prayer and let it go, continually laying it at the feet of Jesus.
   - **If YES**, ask:
2. Is there anything productive* I can do about it?   Yes ☐  No ☐
   (*Consider whether it has potential to repair the issue & whether I will look back on the action with regret.)
   - **If NO**, spend time in prayer and let it go, continually laying it at the feet of Jesus.
   - **If YES**, ask:
3. What can I do, and how can I do it ASAP or implement a long-term plan? _____
   _____
   _____

4. Spend time in prayer and let it go, continually laying it at the feet of Jesus.

My prayer for the day: _____
_____
_____
_____

Random things I'd like to talk about, process, or remember: _____
_____
_____
_____

Today I'm thankful for: _____
_____

Anything about today that was:
True: _____
Honorable: _____
Pure: _____
Lovely: _____
Admirable: _____
Excellent: _____
Worthy of Praise: _____

A negative thought/lie I'm trying to retrain is: _____
_____
_____
_____

A Bible verse to teach myself the truth when that thought/lie arises is:
_____
_____
_____

A song, Bible verse, or quote I'm going to ponder throughout the day is:
_____
_____
_____

Successes, progress, or things I learned today: _____
_____
_____

**A negative emotion I battled today was:** _____

1. Was it appropriate to the situation*?  Yes ☐  No ☐
   (*Consider whether it was a real issue or influenced by mood, circumstance, or prior events.)
   - **If NO,** spend time in prayer and let it go, continually laying it at the feet of Jesus.
   - **If YES,** ask:
2. Is there anything productive* I can do about it?  Yes ☐  No ☐
   (*Consider whether it has potential to repair the issue & whether I will look back on the action with regret.)
   - **If NO,** spend time in prayer and let it go, continually laying it at the feet of Jesus.
   - **If YES,** ask:
3. What can I do, and how can I do it ASAP or implement a long-term plan? _____
_____
_____

4. Spend time in prayer and let it go, continually laying it at the feet of Jesus.

**My prayer for the day:** _____
_____
_____
_____

**Random things I'd like to talk about, process, or remember:** _____
_____
_____
_____

Today I'm thankful for: _____
_____
_____

**Anything about today that was:**
True: _____
Honorable: _____
Pure: _____
Lovely: _____
Admirable: _____
Excellent: _____
Worthy of Praise: _____

A negative thought/lie I'm trying to retrain is: _____
_____
_____
_____

A Bible verse to teach myself the truth when that thought/lie arises is:
_____
_____
_____

A song, Bible verse, or quote I'm going to ponder throughout the day is:
_____
_____
_____

Successes, progress, or things I learned today: _____
_____
_____

**A negative emotion I battled today was:** _____

1. **Was it appropriate to the situation*?** Yes ☐ No ☐
   (*Consider whether it was a real issue or influenced by mood, circumstance, or prior events.)
   - **If NO**, spend time in prayer and let it go, continually laying it at the feet of Jesus.
   - **If YES**, ask:
2. **Is there anything productive* I can do about it?** Yes ☐ No ☐
   (*Consider whether it has potential to repair the issue & whether I will look back on the action with regret.)
   - **If NO**, spend time in prayer and let it go, continually laying it at the feet of Jesus.
   - **If YES**, ask:
3. **What can I do, and how can I do it ASAP or implement a long-term plan?** _____
   _____
   _____

4. Spend time in prayer and let it go, continually laying it at the feet of Jesus.

**My prayer for the day:** _____
_____
_____
_____

**Random things I'd like to talk about, process, or remember:** _____
_____
_____
_____

Today I'm thankful for: _____
_____
_____

**Anything about today that was:**
True: _____
Honorable: _____
Pure: _____
Lovely: _____
Admirable: _____
Excellent: _____
Worthy of Praise: _____

A negative thought/lie I'm trying to retrain is: _____
_____
_____
_____

A Bible verse to teach myself the truth when that thought/lie arises is:
_____
_____
_____

A song, Bible verse, or quote I'm going to ponder throughout the day is:
_____
_____
_____

Successes, progress, or things I learned today: _____
_____
_____

A negative emotion I battled today was: _____

1. Was it appropriate to the situation*?  Yes ☐  No ☐
   (*Consider whether it was a real issue or influenced by mood, circumstance, or prior events.)
   - **If NO**, spend time in prayer and let it go, continually laying it at the feet of Jesus.
   - **If YES**, ask:
2. Is there anything productive* I can do about it?  Yes ☐  No ☐
   (*Consider whether it has potential to repair the issue & whether I will look back on the action with regret.)
   - **If NO**, spend time in prayer and let it go, continually laying it at the feet of Jesus.
   - **If YES**, ask:
3. What can I do, and how can I do it ASAP or implement a long-term plan? _____
   _____
   _____

4. Spend time in prayer and let it go, continually laying it at the feet of Jesus.

My prayer for the day: _____
_____
_____
_____

Random things I'd like to talk about, process, or remember: _____
_____
_____

# Notes

# LIVING AUTHENTIC EXPECTATIONS

I fear that the "Spiritual Motion Sickness" section might've discouraged some of you. It's easy to read it and think, "I would *love* to live my core values and do meaningful things with my time, but you don't understand my work, kids, family, demands, trauma, health struggles...."

I've lived the three-job life, and I know that dwelling on all the things I wanted to do but didn't have the time, money, or ability for would leave me feeling defeated and resentful. During that time, someone encouraging me to write that book I'd always dreamed of would've just felt like a cruel taunt.

We want to do all the things and achieve all the lofty goals, but we often have unrealistic expectations about what we're able to do.

So I'll say it again: we often need to do *less*, not more. We just need to be more intentional about what that "less" includes.

Sometimes—especially on the front end—becoming the person God made us to be requires more internal work than external. We need to heal, rest, learn, grow, and back away from society's obsession with accomplishment.

This may mean we need to pare down our obligations and our to-do lists. There are seasons for learning, internal growth, and strengthening relationships during which it may look like we're doing very little on the outside.

I've been in a season like this for some time. It's been restorative and life-changing but also challenging. I've had to battle my task-completing nature and force myself to be still, accepting that what's going on inside of me is worth time and attention.

## Taking Every Thought Captive

I didn't realize the extent to which I'd placed my value and identity in how much I was able to do and how well I could do it. With that misplaced identity came the fear that others would only see me as lovable if I was useful, constantly meeting needs, and providing something to them or the rest of the world.

Silence and stillness may feel like failure if we've placed our identity in accomplishment, but when our hearts are wounded, exhausted, or empty, then that's what we need to focus on. "Watch over your heart with all diligence, for from it flow the springs of life" (Proverbs 4:23).

If we don't watch over our hearts with diligence, then what flows from them will be something other—and always worse—than "springs of life."

I recently had a conversation with someone who had been overworked for years—working 60-70 hours a week. She was burnt out and overwhelmed. When she was finally able to change jobs, there were many things she wanted to do, but she recognized that her first priority was to give her body and mind the chance to recover from those years. Instead of diving into all the hobbies and activities she'd been missing out on, she focused on getting enough sleep, exercising, and transforming her eating habits. She didn't ask anything else of herself.

We all have times when something similar might be needed in order to give our bodies and minds time to heal, grow, and process.

If you feel overwhelmed, perhaps you could ask yourself what activities or obligations can be relinquished for a time while you focus on your priorities. This might not be popular with some of the people in your life.

Living your values isn't always going to make everyone around you happy. Unfortunately, we often have people in our lives who really do seem only to value us to the degree we're able to accomplish what they expect and desire, but people-pleasing rarely brings inner peace and fulfillment. Instead, it keeps us in an endless race that feels impossible to win.

Remember that Jesus often withdrew from the crowds even when the people wanted more from Him. Focusing where you need to focus doesn't always mean doing what other people want.

## Living Authentic Expectations

But now for a slightly more difficult truth: focusing where you need to focus also doesn't always mean doing what *you* want.

We sometimes mistake our strong desires for core values, but they're not the same thing. I could've lived out my core values whether I'd ever been given the opportunity to write that book I'd dreamed of or not.

Core values are things we can work toward no matter the circumstances in our lives—our character and learning to live the fruit of the Spirit, which is love, joy, peace, patience, kindness, goodness, faithfulness, gentleness, and self-control (Galatians 5:22-23).

"Against such things there is no law," as verse 23 goes on to say. No person, spouse, family member, boss, system, or government can keep me from living those things out.

Living our values may not mean we get to pursue our desires. Jesus wasn't stepping away from the crowds to chase His dreams, but rather to stay aligned with the Father's will and to serve well.

There's nothing wrong with Shawn Achor's example of learning to play the guitar in *The Happiness Advantage*, but it's not truly the guitar playing that represents the core value. It's applying self-discipline to things that matter. It's about bridging the gap between who we are and who we want to be, and that is, first and foremost, someone we can respect.

There are seasons—and for some, entire lifetimes—during which we may not be in control of how we spend our time. Living our values doesn't mean we get to do what we want to the detriment of performing our duties. All our energies may be needed to raise our kids, live a financially responsible life, manage health issues, or care for elderly parents. If we allow the accomplishment of specific tasks to become indicators of how we feel about ourselves and our lives, many of us will never find contentment.

However, if we believe Jesus's words, we can take joy in the fact that to lose our life is to find it (Matthew 10:39, Matthew 16:25). We may never get to learn the guitar or write the book, but we can always be people of integrity, living out the fruit of the Spirit.

Life can impede tasks, but it cannot change who we are…unless we let it.

## Taking Every Thought Captive

Releasing our own personal desires and expectations isn't easy. On the front end, it feels like trading ice cream in for broccoli—a thing we understand the reasoning behind but still aren't excited about. On the back end, however, what we experience is the true joy that a life of earthly fulfillment can never bring—a life built on truth, integrity, and eternal fulfillment.

Instead of chasing the ever-elusive "happiness" the world advertises, we can follow a guaranteed path to joy and purpose.

We'll talk a little more about this in the next section.

"WE OFTEN NEED TO DO LESS, NOT MORE.
WE JUST NEED TO BE MORE INTENTIONAL
ABOUT WHAT THAT "LESS" INCLUDES."

Today I'm thankful for: _____
_____
_____

**Anything about today that was:**
True: _____
Honorable: _____
Pure: _____
Lovely: _____
Admirable: _____
Excellent: _____
Worthy of Praise: _____

A negative thought/lie I'm trying to retrain is: _____
_____
_____
_____

A Bible verse to teach myself the truth when that thought/lie arises is:
_____
_____
_____

A song, Bible verse, or quote I'm going to ponder throughout the day is:
_____
_____
_____

Successes, progress, or things I learned today: _____
_____
_____

**A negative emotion I battled today was:** _____

1. **Was it appropriate to the situation*?**   Yes ☐  No ☐
   (*Consider whether it was a real issue or influenced by mood, circumstance, or prior events.)
   - **If NO**, spend time in prayer and let it go, continually laying it at the feet of Jesus.
   - **If YES**, ask:
2. **Is there anything productive* I can do about it?**   Yes ☐  No ☐
   (*Consider whether it has potential to repair the issue & whether I will look back on the action with regret.)
   - **If NO**, spend time in prayer and let it go, continually laying it at the feet of Jesus.
   - **If YES**, ask:
3. **What can I do, and how can I do it ASAP or implement a long-term plan?** _____
   _____
   _____

4. **Spend time in prayer and let it go, continually laying it at the feet of Jesus.**

**My prayer for the day:** _____
_____
_____
_____

**Random things I'd like to talk about, process, or remember:** _____
_____
_____
_____

Today I'm thankful for: _____
_____
_____

**Anything about today that was:**
True: _____
Honorable: _____
Pure: _____
Lovely: _____
Admirable: _____
Excellent: _____
Worthy of Praise: _____

**A negative thought/lie I'm trying to retrain is:** ___
_____
_____
_____

**A Bible verse to teach myself the truth when that thought/lie arises is:**
_____
_____
_____

**A song, Bible verse, or quote I'm going to ponder throughout the day is:**
_____
_____
_____

**Successes, progress, or things I learned today:** ___
_____
_____

**A negative emotion I battled today was:** _____

1. **Was it appropriate to the situation*?**   Yes ☐   No ☐
   (*Consider whether it was a real issue or influenced by mood, circumstance, or prior events.)
   - **If NO**, spend time in prayer and let it go, continually laying it at the feet of Jesus.
   - **If YES**, ask:
2. **Is there anything productive* I can do about it?**  Yes ☐   No ☐
   (*Consider whether it has potential to repair the issue & whether I will look back on the action with regret.)
   - **If NO**, spend time in prayer and let it go, continually laying it at the feet of Jesus.
   - **If YES**, ask:
3. What can I do, and how can I do it ASAP or implement a long-term plan? _____
   _____
   _____

4. Spend time in prayer and let it go, continually laying it at the feet of Jesus.

**My prayer for the day:** _____
_____
_____
_____

**Random things I'd like to talk about, process, or remember:** _____
_____
_____
_____

Today I'm thankful for: _____
_____
_____

Anything about today that was:
True: _____
Honorable: _____
Pure: _____
Lovely: _____
Admirable: _____
Excellent: _____
Worthy of Praise: _____

A negative thought/lie I'm trying to retrain is: _____
_____
_____
_____

A Bible verse to teach myself the truth when that thought/lie arises is:
_____
_____
_____

A song, Bible verse, or quote I'm going to ponder throughout the day is:
_____
_____
_____

Successes, progress, or things I learned today: _____
_____
_____

**A negative emotion I battled today was:** _____

1. Was it appropriate to the situation*?    Yes ☐  No ☐
   (*Consider whether it was a real issue or influenced by mood, circumstance, or prior events.)
   - **If NO**, spend time in prayer and let it go, continually laying it at the feet of Jesus.
   - **If YES**, ask:
2. Is there anything productive* I can do about it?    Yes ☐  No ☐
   (*Consider whether it has potential to repair the issue & whether I will look back on the action with regret.)
   - **If NO**, spend time in prayer and let it go, continually laying it at the feet of Jesus.
   - **If YES**, ask:
3. What can I do, and how can I do it ASAP or implement a long-term plan? _____
   _____
   _____

4. Spend time in prayer and let it go, continually laying it at the feet of Jesus.

**My prayer for the day:** _____
_____
_____
_____

**Random things I'd like to talk about, process, or remember:** _____
_____
_____
_____

Today I'm thankful for: _____

Anything about today that was:
True: _____
Honorable: _____
Pure: _____
Lovely: _____
Admirable: _____
Excellent: _____
Worthy of Praise: _____

A negative thought/lie I'm trying to retrain is: _____

A Bible verse to teach myself the truth when that thought/lie arises is: _____

A song, Bible verse, or quote I'm going to ponder throughout the day is: _____

Successes, progress, or things I learned today: _____

**A negative emotion I battled today was:** _____

1. **Was it appropriate to the situation*?**   Yes ☐  No ☐
   (*Consider whether it was a real issue or influenced by mood, circumstance, or prior events.)
   - **If NO**, spend time in prayer and let it go, continually laying it at the feet of Jesus.
   - **If YES**, ask:
2. **Is there anything productive* I can do about it?**  Yes ☐  No ☐
   (*Consider whether it has potential to repair the issue & whether I will look back on the action with regret.)
   - **If NO**, spend time in prayer and let it go, continually laying it at the feet of Jesus.
   - **If YES**, ask:
3. **What can I do, and how can I do it ASAP or implement a long-term plan?** _____
   _____
   _____

4. **Spend time in prayer and let it go, continually laying it at the feet of Jesus.**

**My prayer for the day:** _____
_____
_____
_____

**Random things I'd like to talk about, process, or remember:** _____
_____
_____
_____

Today I'm thankful for: _____
_____
_____

Anything about today that was:
True: _____
Honorable: _____
Pure: _____
Lovely: _____
Admirable: _____
Excellent: _____
Worthy of Praise: _____

A negative thought/lie I'm trying to retrain is: _____
_____
_____
_____

A Bible verse to teach myself the truth when that thought/lie arises is:
_____
_____
_____

A song, Bible verse, or quote I'm going to ponder throughout the day is:
_____
_____
_____

Successes, progress, or things I learned today: _____
_____
_____

**A negative emotion I battled today was:** _____

1. **Was it appropriate to the situation*?**  Yes ☐  No ☐
   (*Consider whether it was a real issue or influenced by mood, circumstance, or prior events.)
   - **If NO**, spend time in prayer and let it go, continually laying it at the feet of Jesus.
   - **If YES**, ask:
2. **Is there anything productive* I can do about it?**  Yes ☐  No ☐
   (*Consider whether it has potential to repair the issue & whether I will look back on the action with regret.)
   - **If NO**, spend time in prayer and let it go, continually laying it at the feet of Jesus.
   - **If YES**, ask:
3. What can I do, and how can I do it ASAP or implement a long-term plan? _____
   _____
   _____

4. Spend time in prayer and let it go, continually laying it at the feet of Jesus.

**My prayer for the day:** _____
_____
_____
_____

**Random things I'd like to talk about, process, or remember:** _____
_____
_____
_____

Today I'm thankful for: _____
_____
_____

Anything about today that was:
True: _____
Honorable: _____
Pure: _____
Lovely: _____
Admirable: _____
Excellent: _____
Worthy of Praise: _____

A negative thought/lie I'm trying to retrain is: _____
_____
_____
_____

A Bible verse to teach myself the truth when that thought/lie arises is:
_____
_____
_____

A song, Bible verse, or quote I'm going to ponder throughout the day is:
_____
_____
_____

Successes, progress, or things I learned today: _____
_____
_____

A negative emotion I battled today was: _____

1. Was it appropriate to the situation*?   Yes ☐  No ☐
   (*Consider whether it was a real issue or influenced by mood, circumstance, or prior events.)
   - **If NO**, spend time in prayer and let it go, continually laying it at the feet of Jesus.
   - **If YES**, ask:
2. Is there anything productive* I can do about it?  Yes ☐  No ☐
   (*Consider whether it has potential to repair the issue & whether I will look back on the action with regret.)
   - **If NO**, spend time in prayer and let it go, continually laying it at the feet of Jesus.
   - **If YES**, ask:
3. What can I do, and how can I do it ASAP or implement a long-term plan? _____
   _____
   _____

4. Spend time in prayer and let it go, continually laying it at the feet of Jesus.

My prayer for the day: _____
_____
_____
_____

Random things I'd like to talk about, process, or remember: _____
_____
_____

Today I'm thankful for: _____
_____
_____

**Anything about today that was:**
True: _____
Honorable: _____
Pure: _____
Lovely: _____
Admirable: _____
Excellent: _____
Worthy of Praise: _____

A negative thought/lie I'm trying to retrain is: _____
_____
_____
_____

A Bible verse to teach myself the truth when that thought/lie arises is:
_____
_____
_____

A song, Bible verse, or quote I'm going to ponder throughout the day is:
_____
_____
_____

Successes, progress, or things I learned today: _____
_____
_____

**A negative emotion I battled today was:** _____

1. **Was it appropriate to the situation*?**   Yes ☐  No ☐
   (*Consider whether it was a real issue or influenced by mood, circumstance, or prior events.)
   - **If NO**, spend time in prayer and let it go, continually laying it at the feet of Jesus.
   - **If YES**, ask:
2. **Is there anything productive* I can do about it?**  Yes ☐  No ☐
   (*Consider whether it has potential to repair the issue & whether I will look back on the action with regret.)
   - **If NO**, spend time in prayer and let it go, continually laying it at the feet of Jesus.
   - **If YES**, ask:
3. What can I do, and how can I do it ASAP or implement a long-term plan? _____
   _____
   _____

4. Spend time in prayer and let it go, continually laying it at the feet of Jesus.

**My prayer for the day:** _____
_____
_____

**Random things I'd like to talk about, process, or remember:** _____
_____
_____
_____

# Notes

# Letting Go of Our Own Agenda

So how do we live a life that reflects authentic, realistic, godly expectations? One that isn't dependent upon our own desires, hopes, or dreams being fulfilled in this lifetime?

It's not easy; trust me, I know. I spent much of my life dissatisfied because of my circumstances. I resented having to work jobs I didn't care about and having to do everyday things I saw as menial. I resented that life was hard.

I felt like if I could only leave all that trivial stuff to other people and be given freedom and time, I could do something that *really* mattered.

This mindset kept me in the bondage of bitterness for years. My belief that "I deserved" led me into sinful actions to try and get what I wanted and sinful attitudes when I didn't get it. It also disrupted any chance of enjoying the life I did have or of being an effective representative for Christ.

I definitely wasn't doing all my work as if I were working for the Lord (Colossians 3:23-24). I was living in an attitude of arrogance, bitterness, resentment, anxiety, and irritation.

A few core concepts helped change this for me.

### ~ GOD IS IN THE INTERRUPTIONS ~

Let's get really personal and talk about our agendas—those sacred to-do lists that shall not be violated!

Okay, okay...maybe this is just me. No? Whew.

I'm a list maniac. I have lists within lists, and I have invisible lists in my head for when I'm not working on those lists. "Free time" doesn't exist for me. In the unlikely event that I should finish my to-do list more quickly than expected, there's something in the queue I intend to do next. I haven't been bored since I was nine.

This is why I don't like last-minute plans. They disrupt the tasks living in my head even if I had nothing on the calendar.

But the Lord has worked with me in this area...a LOT. I could write a book about the process. Maybe one day, I will. But for now, it can be summed up in this thought:

I don't know where my time is best spent, but God does. I could order my days to microscopic precision with tasks I deem meaningful, and it might all be worthless in the long run.

The truth is, it's very easy to be busy without being purposeful. So I've learned—very slowly and painfully—to trust God when my schedule is disrupted.

Life requires things of us, and God knows what we need to be doing. Sometimes those things aren't what we intended, and many times, they're nothing we could've even imagined.

In *The Collected Letters of C.S. Lewis, Volume II*, Lewis says, "The great thing, if one can, is to stop regarding all the unpleasant things as interruptions of one's 'own', or 'real' life. The truth is of course that what one calls the interruptions are precisely one's real life–the life God is sending one day by day: what one calls one's 'real life' is a phantom of one's own imagination. This at least is what I see at moments of insight: but it's hard to remember it all the time."

It took me a long time to realize that if I resent the interruptions, I'm *resenting my life*. And isn't that what we're talking about here? Learning to live the lives we have with authentic expectations rather than coveting the lives we *imagine* we should have?

Maybe I planned to work on this project all day—something I believe to be God's will and hope will be helpful and healing to others—but I realize mid-morning that there are really too many outstanding home and business tasks I can't put off. I can become disgruntled and put out, or I can live my life and do what it requires.

Or maybe a friend messages me with a need, and I spend two hours encouraging or praying with her. If I'm doing that with resentment

## Letting Go Of Our Own Agenda

because I've been pulled away from my intended task rather than with love, I may as well be banging pots in her face (1 Corinthians 13:1).

Maybe your car broke down. Maybe your child woke up sick. Maybe...well, maybe anything. Life is full of interruptions.

What I see now is that if I can't bring God with me into the interruptions, I'm setting my own agenda up as a little god in my life—allowing it to control whether I live out the fruit of the Spirit or not.

If I can't accept regular administrative duties and the needs of people I love with grace, how would I ever walk through true persecution and suffering with godliness (1 Peter 4:12-19)?

But when I believe that God is also in the interruptions, He makes them meaningful. My interactions can be fueled by the Holy Spirit then as much as when I'm doing what I consider the important work.

And according to the Word, my idea of "important work" is likely quite skewed.

The disciples thought that Jesus's work was too important for him to be interrupted by children, but He disagreed (Luke 18:15-16).

1 Corinthians 10:31 says, "Therefore, whether you eat or drink, or whatever you do, do all things for the glory of God."

"*Whatever* you do..."

There is no sacred vs. secular. If I can eat or drink to the glory of God, then I can also cook dinner, take the car to the mechanic, and perform that unexpected work task to the glory of God.

I can trust that my times are in His hands (Psalm 31:15) and that as I follow Him, He will always give me exactly enough time to do what He has for me to do...but not necessarily what I think I should do. The trick is that we must be walking with Him to know the difference. In her book *Secure in the Everlasting Arms*, Elisabeth Elliot said, "There is always time to do the will of God. If we are too busy to do that, we are too busy."

Following Him and shifting gears when needed often means I don't accomplish as much as I'd intended according to my own agenda. The truth is that necessity often requires shifting gears whether I'm paying attention to His guidance or not, and I can do that with grace or I can do it with irritation.

Accepting the interruptions that cross my path with grace and love means that even when my to-do list is still full, I have lived my life well, imbuing each task with eternal value. That's how we can do everything to His glory.

### ~ CIRCUMSTANCES CAN'T AFFECT OUR WORTH ~

Oswald Chambers said, "Wherever the providence of God may dump us down, in a slum, in a shop, in the desert, we have to labour along the line of His direction. Never allow this thought—'I am of no use where I am,' because you certainly can be of no use where you are not! Wherever He has engineered your circumstances, pray."[2]

How beautifully simple that statement is! Of course I can only be useful where I am and never where I am not!

If I think I must wait to live a purposeful, godly life till my circumstances are just as I imagined, I will never live a purposeful, godly life (Luke 16:10-11).

The circumstances may be chosen for me, but I'm still told to live my life faithfully. As Paul said, "Are you a slave? Don't worry about it. What matters is keeping God's Word" (my paraphrase of 1 Corinthians 7:19-21). He says similar things in 1 Timothy 6:1.

It doesn't mean we have to live as slaves forever (or in my case, remain in jobs I didn't like forever)—the passage immediately goes on to say that if you can become free, do so—but it does mean that being in a difficult place we did not choose and do not like doesn't impede our ability to do right by the Lord's standards. We can always be the Christians He made us to be no matter what circumstances we may have to endure.

Joseph fulfilled a purpose in slavery and prison. Moses fulfilled a purpose despite his inability to speak well. Ruth fulfilled a purpose as a poor, widowed foreigner. Esther fulfilled a purpose in a forced marriage to an unbelieving king. Paul fulfilled a purpose while being beaten,

---

2   *So Send I You*, Oswald Chambers

stoned, persecuted, and shipwrecked. Jesus fulfilled a purpose while being murdered.

If even a death sentence can't impede our purpose for the Lord when we're following Him, neither can bad bosses, never-ending laundry, overwhelming anxiety, disabilities, health struggles, or having a child with special needs.

But this does require something of us. 2 Timothy 2:20-21 says, "Now in a large house there are not only gold and silver implements, but also implements of wood and of earthenware, and some are for honor while others are for dishonor. Therefore, if anyone cleanses himself from these things, he will be an implement for honor, sanctified, useful to the Master, prepared for every good work."

Our lives will be used for the Lord's purpose regardless, but we get to choose whether He uses us for honorable or dishonorable work. It says we must cleanse ourselves of "these things," and mentions wickedness, youthful lusts, worldly talk, foolish disputes, and being argumentative, among other things.

If we want our lives to have a positive impact, our first thought shouldn't be that our circumstances must change, but that *we* must change. We must "pursue righteousness, faith, love, and peace," as the very next verse says (2 Timothy 2:22).

## ~ NOTHING IS WASTED ~

This concept builds on the last—it's the biblical truth that we can serve God faithfully in the middle of difficult circumstances, and that, for us as believers, God will use ALL those difficult things for good.

Romans 8:28 says, "And we know that God causes all things to work together for good to those who love God, to those who are called according to His purpose."

"We know...." We don't have to wonder if this is true.

"All things...." Yes, that means EVERYTHING that happens to us—the good, the bad, and the ugly.

The only condition is that this is for those who love God. If we don't love God and seek His purposes, there's no guarantee that trials will be transformed in our lives. He's the one who transforms them, but we must let Him work in our lives and our hearts.

Would Joseph's slavery and imprisonment have resulted in his ability to save nations from famine if he had not loved the Lord through it? Would we have ever heard of Ruth if she hadn't shown such loyalty to her mother-in-law? What if Esther had chosen not to confront the King about the plot to eradicate the Jews?

Mordecai's words to her remind us, "If you keep silent at this time, liberation and rescue will arise for the Jews from another place, and you and your father's house will perish. And who knows whether you have not attained royalty for such a time as this?" (Esther 4:14)

God could have transformed those events whether Joseph, Ruth, or Esther chose to live faithfully through them or not, but they likely wouldn't have been transformed in the lives of Joseph, Ruth, or Esther. He could have raised someone else up to accomplish His purpose, but Joseph might've languished in prison for the rest of his life, Ruth might've lived the rest of her life lonely in a godless land, and Esther might've perished needlessly.

The important thing to remember is that this verse doesn't say that all things *are* good. It says that God will *use* all things for good. Don't ever let anyone tell you that evil, trauma, pain, or tragedy are good things.

But we don't have to live in despair because of the terrible things that may happen in our lives or in the world because we *know* that God will transform them for those who love Him. He will make beauty from ashes, and He will bring gladness from mourning (Isaiah 61:3).

Follow Him, and all will be redeemed. Every cruelty borne without bitterness, every harsh word returned with gentleness, every overwhelming task performed with integrity, every injustice endured with patience, and every endeavor undertaken for peace in the face of hatred will yield unimaginable blessings. Don't follow Him, and cruelty is just cruel, harsh words are just harsh, overwhelming tasks are just overwhelming....

"Blessed are the poor in spirit, for theirs is the kingdom of heaven. Blessed are those who mourn, for they will be comforted. Blessed are the gentle, for they will inherit the earth. Blessed are those who hunger and

## Letting Go Of Our Own Agenda

thirst for righteousness, for they will be satisfied. Blessed are the merciful, for they will receive mercy. Blessed are the pure in heart, for they will see God. Blessed are the peacemakers, for they will be called sons of God. Blessed are those who have been persecuted for the sake of righteousness, for theirs is the kingdom of heaven. Blessed are you when people insult you and persecute you, and falsely say all kinds of evil against you because of Me. Rejoice and be glad, for your reward in heaven is great; for in this same way they persecuted the prophets who were before you" (Matthew 5:3-11).

Today I'm thankful for: _____
_____
_____

**Anything about today that was:**
True: _____
Honorable: _____
Pure: _____
Lovely: _____
Admirable: _____
Excellent: _____
Worthy of Praise: _____

A negative thought/lie I'm trying to retrain is: _____
_____
_____
_____

A Bible verse to teach myself the truth when that thought/lie arises is:
_____
_____
_____

A song, Bible verse, or quote I'm going to ponder throughout the day is:
_____
_____
_____

Successes, progress, or things I learned today: _____
_____
_____

A negative emotion I battled today was: _____

1. Was it appropriate to the situation*?  Yes ☐  No ☐
   (*Consider whether it was a real issue or influenced by mood, circumstance, or prior events.)
   - **If NO**, spend time in prayer and let it go, continually laying it at the feet of Jesus.
   - **If YES**, ask:
2. Is there anything productive* I can do about it?  Yes ☐  No ☐
   (*Consider whether it has potential to repair the issue & whether I will look back on the action with regret.)
   - **If NO**, spend time in prayer and let it go, continually laying it at the feet of Jesus.
   - **If YES**, ask:
3. What can I do, and how can I do it ASAP or implement a long-term plan? _____
   _____
   _____

4. Spend time in prayer and let it go, continually laying it at the feet of Jesus.

My prayer for the day: _____
_____
_____
_____

Random things I'd like to talk about, process, or remember: _____
_____
_____
_____

Today I'm thankful for: _____
_____
_____

Anything about today that was:
True: _____
Honorable: _____
Pure: _____
Lovely: _____
Admirable: _____
Excellent: _____
Worthy of Praise: _____

A negative thought/lie I'm trying to retrain is: _____
_____
_____
_____

A Bible verse to teach myself the truth when that thought/lie arises is:
_____
_____
_____

A song, Bible verse, or quote I'm going to ponder throughout the day is:
_____
_____
_____

Successes, progress, or things I learned today: _____
_____
_____

**A negative emotion I battled today was:** _____

1. **Was it appropriate to the situation\*?**   Yes ☐  No ☐
   (\*Consider whether it was a real issue or influenced by mood, circumstance, or prior events.)
   - **If NO**, spend time in prayer and let it go, continually laying it at the feet of Jesus.
   - **If YES**, ask:
2. **Is there anything productive\* I can do about it?**  Yes ☐  No ☐
   (\*Consider whether it has potential to repair the issue & whether I will look back on the action with regret.)
   - **If NO**, spend time in prayer and let it go, continually laying it at the feet of Jesus.
   - **If YES**, ask:
3. **What can I do, and how can I do it ASAP or implement a long-term plan?** _____
   _____
   _____

4. **Spend time in prayer and let it go, continually laying it at the feet of Jesus.**

**My prayer for the day:** _____
_____
_____
_____

**Random things I'd like to talk about, process, or remember:** _____
_____
_____
_____

Today I'm thankful for: _____
_____
_____

**Anything about today that was:**
True: _____
Honorable: _____
Pure: _____
Lovely: _____
Admirable: _____
Excellent: _____
Worthy of Praise: _____

**A negative thought/lie I'm trying to retrain is:** _____
_____
_____
_____

**A Bible verse to teach myself the truth when that thought/lie arises is:**
_____
_____
_____

**A song, Bible verse, or quote I'm going to ponder throughout the day is:**
_____
_____
_____

**Successes, progress, or things I learned today:** _____
_____
_____

**A negative emotion I battled today was:** _____

1. **Was it appropriate to the situation*?** Yes ☐ No ☐
   (*Consider whether it was a real issue or influenced by mood, circumstance, or prior events.)
   - **If NO**, spend time in prayer and let it go, continually laying it at the feet of Jesus.
   - **If YES**, ask:
2. **Is there anything productive* I can do about it?** Yes ☐ No ☐
   (*Consider whether it has potential to repair the issue & whether I will look back on the action with regret.)
   - **If NO**, spend time in prayer and let it go, continually laying it at the feet of Jesus.
   - **If YES**, ask:
3. **What can I do, and how can I do it ASAP or implement a long-term plan?** _____
   _____
   _____

4. Spend time in prayer and let it go, continually laying it at the feet of Jesus.

**My prayer for the day:** _____
_____
_____
_____

**Random things I'd like to talk about, process, or remember:** _____
_____
_____
_____

Today I'm thankful for: _____
_____
_____

**Anything about today that was:**
True: _____
Honorable: _____
Pure: _____
Lovely: _____
Admirable: _____
Excellent: _____
Worthy of Praise: _____

A negative thought/lie I'm trying to retrain is: _____
_____
_____
_____

A Bible verse to teach myself the truth when that thought/lie arises is:
_____
_____
_____

A song, Bible verse, or quote I'm going to ponder throughout the day is:
_____
_____
_____

Successes, progress, or things I learned today: _____
_____
_____

A negative emotion I battled today was: _____

1. Was it appropriate to the situation*?   Yes ☐   No ☐
   (*Consider whether it was a real issue or influenced by mood, circumstance, or prior events.)
   - **If NO**, spend time in prayer and let it go, continually laying it at the feet of Jesus.
   - **If YES**, ask:
2. Is there anything productive* I can do about it?   Yes ☐   No ☐
   (*Consider whether it has potential to repair the issue & whether I will look back on the action with regret.)
   - **If NO**, spend time in prayer and let it go, continually laying it at the feet of Jesus.
   - **If YES**, ask:
3. What can I do, and how can I do it ASAP or implement a long-term plan? _____
   _____
   _____

4. Spend time in prayer and let it go, continually laying it at the feet of Jesus.

My prayer for the day: _____
_____
_____
_____

Random things I'd like to talk about, process, or remember: _____
_____
_____
_____

Today I'm thankful for: _____

**Anything about today that was:**
True: _____
Honorable: _____
Pure: _____
Lovely: _____
Admirable: _____
Excellent: _____
Worthy of Praise: _____

A negative thought/lie I'm trying to retrain is: _____

A Bible verse to teach myself the truth when that thought/lie arises is: _____

A song, Bible verse, or quote I'm going to ponder throughout the day is: _____

Successes, progress, or things I learned today: _____

**A negative emotion I battled today was:** _____

1. **Was it appropriate to the situation*?**  Yes ☐  No ☐
   (*Consider whether it was a real issue or influenced by mood, circumstance, or prior events.)
   - **If NO**, spend time in prayer and let it go, continually laying it at the feet of Jesus.
   - **If YES**, ask:
2. **Is there anything productive* I can do about it?**  Yes ☐  No ☐
   (*Consider whether it has potential to repair the issue & whether I will look back on the action with regret.)
   - **If NO**, spend time in prayer and let it go, continually laying it at the feet of Jesus.
   - **If YES**, ask:
3. **What can I do, and how can I do it ASAP or implement a long-term plan?** _____
   _____
   _____

4. Spend time in prayer and let it go, continually laying it at the feet of Jesus.

**My prayer for the day:** _____
_____
_____
_____

**Random things I'd like to talk about, process, or remember:** _____
_____
_____
_____

Today I'm thankful for: _____
_____
_____

Anything about today that was:
True: _____
Honorable: _____
Pure: _____
Lovely: _____
Admirable: _____
Excellent: _____
Worthy of Praise: _____

A negative thought/lie I'm trying to retrain is: _____
_____
_____
_____

A Bible verse to teach myself the truth when that thought/lie arises is:
_____
_____
_____

A song, Bible verse, or quote I'm going to ponder throughout the day is:
_____
_____
_____

Successes, progress, or things I learned today: _____
_____
_____

**A negative emotion I battled today was:** _____

1. **Was it appropriate to the situation\*?**   Yes ☐  No ☐
   (*Consider whether it was a real issue or influenced by mood, circumstance, or prior events.)
   - **If NO,** spend time in prayer and let it go, continually laying it at the feet of Jesus.
   - **If YES,** ask:
2. **Is there anything productive\* I can do about it?**   Yes ☐  No ☐
   (*Consider whether it has potential to repair the issue & whether I will look back on the action with regret.)
   - **If NO,** spend time in prayer and let it go, continually laying it at the feet of Jesus.
   - **If YES,** ask:
3. **What can I do, and how can I do it ASAP or implement a long-term plan?** _____
   _____
   _____

4. **Spend time in prayer and let it go, continually laying it at the feet of Jesus.**

**My prayer for the day:** _____
_____
_____
_____

**Random things I'd like to talk about, process, or remember:** _____
_____
_____
_____

Today I'm thankful for: _____

Anything about today that was:
True: _____
Honorable: _____
Pure: _____
Lovely: _____
Admirable: _____
Excellent: _____
Worthy of Praise: _____

A negative thought/lie I'm trying to retrain is: _____

A Bible verse to teach myself the truth when that thought/lie arises is:

A song, Bible verse, or quote I'm going to ponder throughout the day is:

Successes, progress, or things I learned today: _____

A negative emotion I battled today was: _____

1. Was it appropriate to the situation*?    Yes ☐  No ☐
   (*Consider whether it was a real issue or influenced by mood, circumstance, or prior events.)
   - **If NO**, spend time in prayer and let it go, continually laying it at the feet of Jesus.
   - **If YES**, ask:
2. Is there anything productive* I can do about it?    Yes ☐  No ☐
   (*Consider whether it has potential to repair the issue & whether I will look back on the action with regret.)
   - **If NO**, spend time in prayer and let it go, continually laying it at the feet of Jesus.
   - **If YES**, ask:
3. What can I do, and how can I do it ASAP or implement a long-term plan? _____
   _____
   _____

4. Spend time in prayer and let it go, continually laying it at the feet of Jesus.

My prayer for the day: _____
_____
_____
_____

Random things I'd like to talk about, process, or remember: _____
_____
_____

**Notes**

# LIVING OUR PURPOSE

We touched on this in the last section, but I want to expand on it, because I know it's really hard to believe that we're valuable no matter what our circumstances look like.

Society and our own expectations have given us the idea that to have meaningful lives, we have to be or do some specific thing.

Maybe you believe your purpose is to be a parent or a spouse, a doctor or a singer, or to be a CEO or take a gold medal in the Olympics.

While all those things are good and you can do them *with* purpose, they are not your purpose as a human being.

God never speaks of purpose in the context of *what* you are, but always in the context of *who* you are.

We often lament, "I just don't know what God wants me to do with my life!"

But, "He has told you, mortal one, what is good; and what does the Lord require of you but to do justice, to love kindness, and to walk humbly with your God?" (Micah 6:8)

The Bible says to live the fruit of the Spirit (Galatians 5:22–23), and as we've already discussed, no one can take away our ability to do this.

It says to go and make disciples, which any of us can do right where we are (Matthew 28:19–20).

It tells us to care for the widows and orphans and to keep away from the world's wickedness (James 1:27). This is not something exclusive to the privileged.

And the greatest commandment of all is "to love God with all our heart, soul, and mind and to love our neighbors as ourselves" (Matthew 22:36–40).

God has already told us what to do with our lives; it's right here in these verses.

Obeying Him in these things might *lead* us to become parents, spouses, doctors, singers, CEOs, or Olympic gold medalists, but that's not where we begin. That will flow from walking out all the other things He's asked of us.

Seek first His kingdom and righteousness; everything else springs from that (Matthew 6:33).

This isn't new knowledge. Solomon—commonly considered the wisest man who ever lived—summed it up this way after studying, experimenting, and philosophizing for years: "The conclusion, when everything has been heard, is: fear God and keep His commandments, because this applies to every person" (Ecclesiastes 12:13).

"*This applies to every person.*"

And there, Solomon hits on the most beautiful thing about God's will for us: absolutely everyone can do it—janitors, teachers, single parents, CEOs, whether chronically ill or healthy, lonely or surrounded by a loving community, poor or rich, weak or strong.

No one is left out where true purpose is concerned, but if "fearing God and keeping His commandments" isn't our aim, everything we do along the way is pointless, as Solomon also reminds us. In Ecclesiastes chapters 1 and 2, he tells us he tried to find meaning in knowledge, pleasure, possessions, wealth, and in his work.

All of it left him feeling empty. He tried everything most of us would include on a list of things we think would ensure happy lives, and none of it worked.

I call this the, "Is that it?" factor. Have you ever taken some major step or hit a big milestone and instead of the lasting euphoria you expected, you felt deflated? Or maybe that feeling lasted for only a day or a week.

For years, maybe you'd been thinking, "If only I could get married, buy the house, have the kid, get the job, win the award, publish the book, achieve the notoriety, or become wealthy, I could finally relax and be happy."

## Living Our Purpose

It doesn't work. I've hit enough of my "if onlys" to know. And the higher my expectations for what that thing would mean in my life, the harder the "is that it?" factor hits, because I've put my hope where it doesn't belong.

The Bible never ever tells us to put our hope in the things of this world; it only says to hope in God, His salvation, and eternity with Him.

There are many other good things in this life, but none of them can fill the place for hope and meaning all of us have. Earthly blessings are nice additions, but they're never essential to true purpose. If we believe they are, then we need to dethrone an idol.

Without God, the greatest things we can imagine accomplishing will fall flat. With Him, the smallest things we can do are infused with purpose.

Many times, when I start feeling aimless, confused, and devoid of purpose, I suddenly realize that God's already told me to do something, and *I'm not doing it.*

Why would He give me the next step if I haven't shown myself willing to do the first?

When we begin walking in step with the Spirit in this way, we may find that He clearly guides us to a specific job, spouse, or calling in ways we could never have predicted, but we can also quench the Spirit (1 Thessalonians 5:19) by continually choosing what the flesh desires over what the Lord tells us is good (Galatians 5:17).

In the end, living our purpose means living God's will, and we do this by taking His Word seriously and attempting to follow it, or in Solomon's words, fearing God and keeping His commandments.

Ultimately, our Creator doesn't define us by titles, achievements, or roles, but by who we are in Him. The "big things" we aspire to—relationships, careers, and accolades—may flow from following Him, but they aren't the source of our value or fulfillment.

We're told to know God, to love Him and love others, to live out justice and mercy, to follow His Word, to keep away from worldly sin, and to nurture the fruit of the Spirit and let Him guide our steps. Out of these things, everything else good will flow.

## Taking Every Thought Captive

It's not about waiting for a grand revelation; it's about faithfully walking out what He's already shown us.

As we center our lives on these things, we'll discover that true purpose is less about what we achieve and more about who we become in Him. No circumstance can take that away.

"The most beautiful thing about God's will for us is that absolutely everyone can do it—janitors, teachers, single parents, CEOs, whether chronically ill or healthy, lonely or surrounded by a loving community, poor or rich, weak or strong."

Today I'm thankful for: _____
_____
_____

Anything about today that was:
True: _____
Honorable: _____
Pure: _____
Lovely: _____
Admirable: _____
Excellent: _____
Worthy of Praise: _____

A negative thought/lie I'm trying to retrain is: _____
_____
_____
_____

A Bible verse to teach myself the truth when that thought/lie arises is:
_____
_____
_____

A song, Bible verse, or quote I'm going to ponder throughout the day is:
_____
_____
_____

Successes, progress, or things I learned today: _____
_____
_____

A negative emotion I battled today was: _____

1. Was it appropriate to the situation*?   Yes ☐  No ☐
   (*Consider whether it was a real issue or influenced by mood, circumstance, or prior events.)
   - **If NO**, spend time in prayer and let it go, continually laying it at the feet of Jesus.
   - **If YES**, ask:
2. Is there anything productive* I can do about it?   Yes ☐  No ☐
   (*Consider whether it has potential to repair the issue & whether I will look back on the action with regret.)
   - **If NO**, spend time in prayer and let it go, continually laying it at the feet of Jesus.
   - **If YES**, ask:
3. What can I do, and how can I do it ASAP or implement a long-term plan? _____
   _____
   _____

4. Spend time in prayer and let it go, continually laying it at the feet of Jesus.

My prayer for the day: _____
_____
_____
_____

Random things I'd like to talk about, process, or remember: _____
_____
_____
_____

205

Today I'm thankful for: _____
_____
_____

Anything about today that was:
True: _____
Honorable: _____
Pure: _____
Lovely: _____
Admirable: _____
Excellent: _____
Worthy of Praise: _____

A negative thought/lie I'm trying to retrain is: _____
_____
_____
_____

A Bible verse to teach myself the truth when that thought/lie arises is:
_____
_____
_____

A song, Bible verse, or quote I'm going to ponder throughout the day is:
_____
_____
_____

Successes, progress, or things I learned today: _____
_____
_____

A negative emotion I battled today was: _____

1. Was it appropriate to the situation*?   Yes ☐  No ☐
   (*Consider whether it was a real issue or influenced by mood, circumstance, or prior events.)
   - **If NO**, spend time in prayer and let it go, continually laying it at the feet of Jesus.
   - **If YES**, ask:
2. Is there anything productive* I can do about it?  Yes ☐  No ☐
   (*Consider whether it has potential to repair the issue & whether I will look back on the action with regret.)
   - **If NO**, spend time in prayer and let it go, continually laying it at the feet of Jesus.
   - **If YES**, ask:
3. What can I do, and how can I do it ASAP or implement a long-term plan? _____
   _____
   _____

4. Spend time in prayer and let it go, continually laying it at the feet of Jesus.

My prayer for the day: _____
_____
_____
_____

Random things I'd like to talk about, process, or remember: _____
_____
_____
_____

Today I'm thankful for: _____
_____
_____

**Anything about today that was:**
True: _____
Honorable: _____
Pure: _____
Lovely: _____
Admirable: _____
Excellent: _____
Worthy of Praise: _____

**A negative thought/lie I'm trying to retrain is:** _____
_____
_____
_____

**A Bible verse to teach myself the truth when that thought/lie arises is:**
_____
_____
_____

**A song, Bible verse, or quote I'm going to ponder throughout the day is:**
_____
_____
_____

**Successes, progress, or things I learned today:** _____
_____
_____

A negative emotion I battled today was: _____

1. Was it appropriate to the situation*?   Yes ☐  No ☐
   (*Consider whether it was a real issue or influenced by mood, circumstance, or prior events.)
   - **If NO**, spend time in prayer and let it go, continually laying it at the feet of Jesus.
   - **If YES**, ask:

2. Is there anything productive* I can do about it?   Yes ☐  No ☐
   (*Consider whether it has potential to repair the issue & whether I will look back on the action with regret.)
   - **If NO**, spend time in prayer and let it go, continually laying it at the feet of Jesus.
   - **If YES**, ask:

3. What can I do, and how can I do it ASAP or implement a long-term plan? _____
   _____
   _____

4. Spend time in prayer and let it go, continually laying it at the feet of Jesus.

My prayer for the day: _____
_____
_____
_____

Random things I'd like to talk about, process, or remember: _____
_____
_____

Today I'm thankful for: _____
_____
_____

Anything about today that was:
True: _____
Honorable: _____
Pure: _____
Lovely: _____
Admirable: _____
Excellent: _____
Worthy of Praise: _____

A negative thought/lie I'm trying to retrain is: _____
_____
_____
_____

A Bible verse to teach myself the truth when that thought/lie arises is:
_____
_____
_____

A song, Bible verse, or quote I'm going to ponder throughout the day is:
_____
_____
_____

Successes, progress, or things I learned today: _____
_____
_____

**A negative emotion I battled today was:** _____

1. Was it appropriate to the situation*?   Yes ☐  No ☐
   (*Consider whether it was a real issue or influenced by mood, circumstance, or prior events.)
   - **If NO,** spend time in prayer and let it go, continually laying it at the feet of Jesus.
   - **If YES,** ask:
2. Is there anything productive* I can do about it?   Yes ☐  No ☐
   (*Consider whether it has potential to repair the issue & whether I will look back on the action with regret.)
   - **If NO,** spend time in prayer and let it go, continually laying it at the feet of Jesus.
   - **If YES,** ask:
3. What can I do, and how can I do it ASAP or implement a long-term plan?_____
   _____
   _____

4. Spend time in prayer and let it go, continually laying it at the feet of Jesus.

**My prayer for the day:** _____
_____
_____
_____

**Random things I'd like to talk about, process, or remember:** _____
_____
_____
_____

Today I'm thankful for: _____
_____
_____

**Anything about today that was:**
True: _____
Honorable: _____
Pure: _____
Lovely: _____
Admirable: _____
Excellent: _____
Worthy of Praise: _____

A negative thought/lie I'm trying to retrain is: _____
_____
_____
_____

A Bible verse to teach myself the truth when that thought/lie arises is:
_____
_____
_____

A song, Bible verse, or quote I'm going to ponder throughout the day is:
_____
_____
_____

Successes, progress, or things I learned today: _____
_____
_____

A negative emotion I battled today was: _____

1. Was it appropriate to the situation*?   Yes ☐  No ☐
   (*Consider whether it was a real issue or influenced by mood, circumstance, or prior events.)
   - **If NO**, spend time in prayer and let it go, continually laying it at the feet of Jesus.
   - **If YES**, ask:
2. Is there anything productive* I can do about it?  Yes ☐  No ☐
   (*Consider whether it has potential to repair the issue & whether I will look back on the action with regret.)
   - **If NO**, spend time in prayer and let it go, continually laying it at the feet of Jesus.
   - **If YES**, ask:
3. What can I do, and how can I do it ASAP or implement a long-term plan? _____
   _____
   _____

4. Spend time in prayer and let it go, continually laying it at the feet of Jesus.

My prayer for the day: _____
_____
_____
_____

Random things I'd like to talk about, process, or remember: _____
_____
_____
_____

Today I'm thankful for: _____
_____
_____

Anything about today that was:
True: _____
Honorable: _____
Pure: _____
Lovely: _____
Admirable: _____
Excellent: _____
Worthy of Praise: _____

A negative thought/lie I'm trying to retrain is: _____
_____
_____
_____

A Bible verse to teach myself the truth when that thought/lie arises is:
_____
_____
_____

A song, Bible verse, or quote I'm going to ponder throughout the day is:
_____
_____
_____

Successes, progress, or things I learned today: _____
_____
_____

A negative emotion I battled today was: _____

1. Was it appropriate to the situation*?  Yes ☐  No ☐
   (*Consider whether it was a real issue or influenced by mood, circumstance, or prior events.)
   - **If NO**, spend time in prayer and let it go, continually laying it at the feet of Jesus.
   - **If YES**, ask:
2. Is there anything productive* I can do about it?  Yes ☐  No ☐
   (*Consider whether it has potential to repair the issue & whether I will look back on the action with regret.)
   - **If NO**, spend time in prayer and let it go, continually laying it at the feet of Jesus.
   - **If YES**, ask:
3. What can I do, and how can I do it ASAP or implement a long-term plan? _____
   _____
   _____

4. Spend time in prayer and let it go, continually laying it at the feet of Jesus.

My prayer for the day: _____
_____
_____
_____

Random things I'd like to talk about, process, or remember: _____
_____
_____
_____

Today I'm thankful for: _____

**Anything about today that was:**
True: _____
Honorable: _____
Pure: _____
Lovely: _____
Admirable: _____
Excellent: _____
Worthy of Praise: _____

A negative thought/lie I'm trying to retrain is: _____

A Bible verse to teach myself the truth when that thought/lie arises is: _____

A song, Bible verse, or quote I'm going to ponder throughout the day is: _____

Successes, progress, or things I learned today: _____

A negative emotion I battled today was: _____

1. Was it appropriate to the situation*?   Yes ☐  No ☐
   (*Consider whether it was a real issue or influenced by mood, circumstance, or prior events.)
   - **If NO**, spend time in prayer and let it go, continually laying it at the feet of Jesus.
   - **If YES**, ask:
2. Is there anything productive* I can do about it?   Yes ☐  No ☐
   (*Consider whether it has potential to repair the issue & whether I will look back on the action with regret.)
   - **If NO**, spend time in prayer and let it go, continually laying it at the feet of Jesus.
   - **If YES**, ask:
3. What can I do, and how can I do it ASAP or implement a long-term plan? _____
   _____
   _____

4. Spend time in prayer and let it go, continually laying it at the feet of Jesus.

My prayer for the day: _____
_____
_____
_____

Random things I'd like to talk about, process, or remember: _____
_____
_____
_____

# Notes

# Regret vs. Godly Sorrow

Reading about how our true purpose is inextricably linked to following the Lord, many of us might have felt feelings of despair.

We can see all the ways we've been choosing our own desires over God's will, ignoring what God asks of us, allowing harmful beliefs and attitudes to reign in our lives, and disobeying clear commandments in His Word. If that's what leads to true purpose, we've failed. We're doomed.

But that's never true. We all have things we wish we hadn't done. Some are difficult to face.

But it's never too late to become the person God designed us to be and to do the good works He laid out for us (Ephesians 2:10).

"The Lord's acts of mercy indeed do not end, for His compassions do not fail. They are new every morning; great is Your faithfulness" (Lamentations 3:22-23).

So how do we handle the shame we feel?

2 Corinthians 7:10 has a beautiful answer: "For the sorrow that is according to the will of God produces a repentance without regret, leading to salvation, but the sorrow of the world produces death."

As this verse tells us, godly sorrow will produce change—*repentance*. Repentance doesn't just mean we feel bad about something; it means we start doing things differently.

It doesn't mean we will start doing things *perfectly*, but there should be consistent forward motion in the right direction. This leads to salvation.

But have you ever watched someone living in regret and shame? They're filled with despair. It doesn't inspire positive change but rather keeps them bound up in the past. It isn't leading them into life, but death.

## Taking Every Thought Captive

To move forward out of shame, we must first have the proper perspective on ourselves.

Many times, our shame is so great because we had that "ideal image" of ourselves, and we can clearly see how greatly we violated it. To move forward, we first need to see that our imagined ideal wasn't realistic.

Deep down, we believed ourselves to be good, and we can't handle the fact that we didn't live up to that belief.

Do you know who's never surprised by our sin? God. He knew Jonah was going to run. He knew Peter was going to deny Him. He knew David was going to commit adultery and murder. He knew Paul was persecuting Christians and seeking to have them killed.

But He called them anyway.

This is redemption. He came to heal the sick, not the well—to redeem the sinners, not those who believed themselves righteous (Mark 2:17).

He always knew we were capable of terrible things, but He loved us anyway. He sent Jesus to die for us *because* He understood our sinfulness, not in spite of it.

So we look at ourselves as He does; we accept His assessment and His forgiveness. He knew we were sinners and loved us even then (Romans 5:8). He did not write us off as hopeless; he chased us down in love.

If the perfect Creator of the universe can look at us, knowing all our deepest, darkest sins down to the unspoken evil thoughts in our hearts, yet still see someone worth saving, then we can do the same, both for ourselves and others. We must be able to look at all the ugliness and still *believe* Him when He says we are worth it.

Until we can understand our own desperate need for Christ and accept His forgiveness, we'll never let go of the worldly shame and regret.

Without that recognition, we also can't truly love our enemies. It's seeing our own sin as God sees it that allows us to forgive others who don't deserve it.

In Luke 7, we see the most beautiful response to great forgiveness in Mary's example as she pours out her expensive perfume to anoint Christ's feet, washing them with her tears, and drying them with her hair. Others expressed disdain for her actions; why was Jesus letting this

## Regret Vs. Godly Sorrow

sinner touch Him? But Jesus asked them, "A moneylender had two debtors: the one owed five hundred denarii, and the other, fifty. When they were unable to repay, he canceled the debts of both. So which of them will love him more? Her sins, which are many, have been forgiven, for she loved much; but the one who is forgiven little, loves little." (Luke 7:41-42, 47)." Where sin increased, grace abounds all the more (Romans 5:20).

This is how we respond when we see the greatness of our sins—with great love for Christ and gratitude for His mercy, ready and willing to give all we have in response to His great forgiveness and the sacrifice it required.

When I look at the things in my past that I'm ashamed of, I remind myself that God was not surprised by my sin, but He loved and pursued me anyway. I remind myself not to wallow in them and let them keep me stuck—mired in shame and despair.

That's exactly what our Enemy, the Accuser, wants (Zechariah 3:1, Revelation 12:10).

What I do is look at my wrongs honestly and recognize that I'm human. I've made mistakes, and I will make more. I take those things to the feet of Jesus, repent of them, view them as lessons on how to do better from this point forward, and determine if I can make amends for what I've done. Then I live a life full of gratitude for God's forgiveness, loving Him because of His great love for me, and ready to pour out everything I have and everything I am at His feet.

It's easy to pick our shame back up again. Sometimes we have people in our lives who make us feel that we *should* pick it back up and carry it with us forever, but it isn't true. These are some of those things we talked about having to "let go and continually lay at the feet of Jesus."

Shame's only purpose is to make us see our need for the Lord and to bring us into repentance—to bring about change in our hearts and lives. If it's not doing that—or if it's doing something other than that—it's been hijacked by the devil.

Through Jesus, the Lord removes our "filthy garments"—our guilt—and clothes us with "festive garments" and a "clean headband" (Zechariah

3:4–5). We overcome Satan's accusations by the blood of Jesus's sacrifice cleansing us from our sin and the word of our testimony continually reminding us that what Jesus did was enough (Revelation 12:11). He covered our sin and brought us into repentance.

We can know that "If we confess our sins, He is faithful and righteous, so that He will forgive us our sins and cleanse us from all unrighteousness" (1 John 1:9).

Once we can accept all of that and begin to see ourselves as God sees us, I think there's one more hurdle. It's still often very difficult not to look at the past and see all the "wasted time," all the ways we've hurt others, and all the things we've left undone in the Kingdom of God.

We can apologize and repair some things (Matthew 5:23–24 makes it clear that we should), but our actions can't be undone and some consequences are forever.

This is where we must train ourselves yet again to believe the truth that the Lord will restore the years the locust has eaten (Joel 2:25), that He will bring beauty from ashes, and gladness from mourning (Isaiah 61:3). We take courage from Joseph's statement in Genesis 50:20, "As for you, you meant evil against me, but God meant it for good in order to bring about this present result, to keep many people alive."

We know that God weaves even our evil deeds into the tapestry of His plan. We were, for a time, vessels of dishonor in His house, but through Jesus's sacrifice and our repentance, we can be vessels of honor from this point forward (2 Timothy 2:20–22).

This doesn't mean there will be no consequences for sinful actions. We must also take our lesson from David whose child died because of his adultery and murder. But we can see in David both the humble attitude of repentance and acceptance of the consequences of his sin.

He grieved, fasted, and prayed while the child was ill, but as soon as his son died, David returned to his normal duties (2 Samuel 12). In Psalm 51 we find his heart-wrenching, beautiful prayer of repentance in which he also expresses the rightness of God's judgment as well as confidence that God will cleanse him from his guilt. "You are justified when You speak and blameless when You judge.... Purify me with hyssop, and I

## Regret Vs. Godly Sorrow

will be clean; cleanse me, and I will be whiter than snow.... The sacrifices of God are a broken spirit; a broken and a contrite heart, God, You will not despise" (Psalm 51:4, 7,17).

We live as Paul, "I do not regard myself as having taken hold of it yet; but one thing I do: forgetting what lies behind and reaching forward to what lies ahead, I press on toward the goal for the prize of the upward call of God in Christ Jesus" (Philippians 3:13-14).

We are bound up in neither the failures nor the victories of the past, but rather always reaching forward into the continual call of Jesus.

Regret looks backward and keeps us stuck, but godly sorrow moves us forward. It's not about denying our sins or their consequences; it's about letting them drive us to repentance and change. God wants us to be transformed by His grace, not trapped in shame. True repentance leads to life, not despair, because it recognizes that our sins don't define us—God's redemption does.

When we accept His forgiveness, we're freed to press on, not as prisoners of the past, but as vessels of honor, walking in step with His purpose for us. Let the sorrow you feel be the kind that propels you into His arms and His plans, leaving regret behind and embracing the new mercies He offers every day.

Today I'm thankful for: _____
_____
_____

Anything about today that was:
True: _____
Honorable: _____
Pure: _____
Lovely: _____
Admirable: _____
Excellent: _____
Worthy of Praise: _____

A negative thought/lie I'm trying to retrain is: _____
_____
_____
_____

A Bible verse to teach myself the truth when that thought/lie arises is:
_____
_____
_____

A song, Bible verse, or quote I'm going to ponder throughout the day is:
_____
_____
_____

Successes, progress, or things I learned today: _____
_____
_____

A negative emotion I battled today was: _____

1. Was it appropriate to the situation*?   Yes ☐  No ☐
   (*Consider whether it was a real issue or influenced by mood, circumstance, or prior events.)
   - **If NO**, spend time in prayer and let it go, continually laying it at the feet of Jesus.
   - **If YES**, ask:
2. Is there anything productive* I can do about it?   Yes ☐  No ☐
   (*Consider whether it has potential to repair the issue & whether I will look back on the action with regret.)
   - **If NO**, spend time in prayer and let it go, continually laying it at the feet of Jesus.
   - **If YES**, ask:
3. What can I do, and how can I do it ASAP or implement a long-term plan?_____
   _____
   _____

4. Spend time in prayer and let it go, continually laying it at the feet of Jesus.

My prayer for the day:_____
_____
_____
_____

Random things I'd like to talk about, process, or remember:_____
_____
_____
_____

Today I'm thankful for: _____
_____
_____

**Anything about today that was:**
True: _____
Honorable: _____
Pure: _____
Lovely: _____
Admirable: _____
Excellent: _____
Worthy of Praise: _____

A negative thought/lie I'm trying to retrain is: _____
_____
_____
_____

A Bible verse to teach myself the truth when that thought/lie arises is:
_____
_____
_____

A song, Bible verse, or quote I'm going to ponder throughout the day is:
_____
_____
_____

Successes, progress, or things I learned today: _____
_____
_____
_____

A negative emotion I battled today was: _____

1. Was it appropriate to the situation*?   Yes ☐   No ☐
   (*Consider whether it was a real issue or influenced by mood, circumstance, or prior events.)
   - **If NO**, spend time in prayer and let it go, continually laying it at the feet of Jesus.
   - **If YES**, ask:
2. Is there anything productive* I can do about it?   Yes ☐   No ☐
   (*Consider whether it has potential to repair the issue & whether I will look back on the action with regret.)
   - **If NO**, spend time in prayer and let it go, continually laying it at the feet of Jesus.
   - **If YES**, ask:
3. What can I do, and how can I do it ASAP or implement a long-term plan? _____
   _____
   _____

4. Spend time in prayer and let it go, continually laying it at the feet of Jesus.

My prayer for the day: _____
_____
_____
_____

Random things I'd like to talk about, process, or remember: _____
_____
_____
_____

Today I'm thankful for: _____
_____
_____

Anything about today that was:
True: _____
Honorable: _____
Pure: _____
Lovely: _____
Admirable: _____
Excellent: _____
Worthy of Praise: _____

A negative thought/lie I'm trying to retrain is: _____
_____
_____
_____

A Bible verse to teach myself the truth when that thought/lie arises is:
_____
_____
_____

A song, Bible verse, or quote I'm going to ponder throughout the day is:
_____
_____
_____

Successes, progress, or things I learned today: _____
_____
_____

A negative emotion I battled today was: _____

1. Was it appropriate to the situation*?   Yes ☐  No ☐
   (*Consider whether it was a real issue or influenced by mood, circumstance, or prior events.)
   - **If NO**, spend time in prayer and let it go, continually laying it at the feet of Jesus.
   - **If YES**, ask:
2. Is there anything productive* I can do about it?   Yes ☐  No ☐
   (*Consider whether it has potential to repair the issue & whether I will look back on the action with regret.)
   - **If NO**, spend time in prayer and let it go, continually laying it at the feet of Jesus.
   - **If YES**, ask:
3. What can I do, and how can I do it ASAP or implement a long-term plan? _____
   _____
   _____

4. Spend time in prayer and let it go, continually laying it at the feet of Jesus.

My prayer for the day: _____
_____
_____
_____

Random things I'd like to talk about, process, or remember: _____
_____
_____
_____

Today I'm thankful for: _____
_____
_____

**Anything about today that was:**
True: _____
Honorable: _____
Pure: _____
Lovely: _____
Admirable: _____
Excellent: _____
Worthy of Praise: _____

A negative thought/lie I'm trying to retrain is: _____
_____
_____
_____

A Bible verse to teach myself the truth when that thought/lie arises is:
_____
_____
_____

A song, Bible verse, or quote I'm going to ponder throughout the day is:
_____
_____
_____

Successes, progress, or things I learned today: _____
_____
_____

**A negative emotion I battled today was:** _____

1. **Was it appropriate to the situation*?**   Yes ☐   No ☐
   (*Consider whether it was a real issue or influenced by mood, circumstance, or prior events.)
   - **If NO**, spend time in prayer and let it go, continually laying it at the feet of Jesus.
   - **If YES**, ask:
2. **Is there anything productive* I can do about it?**   Yes ☐   No ☐
   (*Consider whether it has potential to repair the issue & whether I will look back on the action with regret.)
   - **If NO**, spend time in prayer and let it go, continually laying it at the feet of Jesus.
   - **If YES**, ask:
3. **What can I do, and how can I do it ASAP or implement a long-term plan?** _____
   _____
   _____

4. **Spend time in prayer and let it go, continually laying it at the feet of Jesus.**

**My prayer for the day:** _____
_____
_____
_____

**Random things I'd like to talk about, process, or remember:** _____
_____
_____

Today I'm thankful for: _____
_____
_____

Anything about today that was:
True: _____
Honorable: _____
Pure: _____
Lovely: _____
Admirable: _____
Excellent: _____
Worthy of Praise: _____

A negative thought/lie I'm trying to retrain is: _____
_____
_____
_____

A Bible verse to teach myself the truth when that thought/lie arises is:
_____
_____
_____

A song, Bible verse, or quote I'm going to ponder throughout the day is:
_____
_____
_____

Successes, progress, or things I learned today: _____
_____
_____

**A negative emotion I battled today was:** _____

1. **Was it appropriate to the situation*?**  Yes ☐  No ☐
   (*Consider whether it was a real issue or influenced by mood, circumstance, or prior events.)
   - **If NO**, spend time in prayer and let it go, continually laying it at the feet of Jesus.
   - **If YES**, ask:
2. **Is there anything productive* I can do about it?**  Yes ☐  No ☐
   (*Consider whether it has potential to repair the issue & whether I will look back on the action with regret.)
   - **If NO**, spend time in prayer and let it go, continually laying it at the feet of Jesus.
   - **If YES**, ask:
3. What can I do, and how can I do it ASAP or implement a long-term plan? _____
   _____
   _____

4. Spend time in prayer and let it go, continually laying it at the feet of Jesus.

**My prayer for the day:** _____
_____
_____
_____

**Random things I'd like to talk about, process, or remember:** _____
_____
_____
_____

Today I'm thankful for: _____

Anything about today that was:
True: _____
Honorable: _____
Pure: _____
Lovely: _____
Admirable: _____
Excellent: _____
Worthy of Praise: _____

A negative thought/lie I'm trying to retrain is: _____

A Bible verse to teach myself the truth when that thought/lie arises is: _____

A song, Bible verse, or quote I'm going to ponder throughout the day is: _____

Successes, progress, or things I learned today: _____

A negative emotion I battled today was: ───────────

1. Was it appropriate to the situation*?    Yes ☐  No ☐
   (*Consider whether it was a real issue or influenced by mood, circumstance, or prior events.)
   - **If NO**, spend time in prayer and let it go, continually laying it at the feet of Jesus.
   - **If YES**, ask:
2. Is there anything productive* I can do about it?  Yes ☐  No ☐
   (*Consider whether it has potential to repair the issue & whether I will look back on the action with regret.)
   - **If NO**, spend time in prayer and let it go, continually laying it at the feet of Jesus.
   - **If YES**, ask:
3. What can I do, and how can I do it ASAP or implement a long-term plan? ───────────
   ───────────
   ───────────

4. Spend time in prayer and let it go, continually laying it at the feet of Jesus.

My prayer for the day: ───────────
───────────
───────────
───────────

Random things I'd like to talk about, process, or remember: ───────────
───────────
───────────
───────────

Today I'm thankful for: _____
_____
_____

**Anything about today that was:**
True: _____
Honorable: _____
Pure: _____
Lovely: _____
Admirable: _____
Excellent: _____
Worthy of Praise: _____

A negative thought/lie I'm trying to retrain is: _____
_____
_____
_____

A Bible verse to teach myself the truth when that thought/lie arises is:
_____
_____
_____

A song, Bible verse, or quote I'm going to ponder throughout the day is:
_____
_____
_____

Successes, progress, or things I learned today: _____
_____
_____

**A negative emotion I battled today was:** _____

1. Was it appropriate to the situation*?   Yes ☐  No ☐
   (*Consider whether it was a real issue or influenced by mood, circumstance, or prior events.)
   - If **NO**, spend time in prayer and let it go, continually laying it at the feet of Jesus.
   - If **YES**, ask:
2. Is there anything productive* I can do about it?   Yes ☐  No ☐
   (*Consider whether it has potential to repair the issue & whether I will look back on the action with regret.)
   - If **NO**, spend time in prayer and let it go, continually laying it at the feet of Jesus.
   - If **YES**, ask:
3. What can I do, and how can I do it ASAP or implement a long-term plan? _____
   _____
   _____

4. Spend time in prayer and let it go, continually laying it at the feet of Jesus.

**My prayer for the day:** _____
_____
_____
_____

**Random things I'd like to talk about, process, or remember:** _____
_____
_____
_____

## Notes

# Comparison

**W**e've all heard the phrase, "Comparison is the thief of joy." That's true, but the harm comparison does goes much further. It also hinders love, inhibits gratitude, creates dissatisfaction, and keeps us focused on ourselves.

Let's start with looking at how comparison is handled in the body of Christ.

God gives different gifts, different callings, and different outcomes (1 Corinthians 12:4-6). They are dispersed exactly as God intends (1 Corinthians 12:11) for the good of all His children (1 Corinthians 12:7). If I look at myself and say, "I'm not good at making people feel comfortable, so I don't fit into the body," that doesn't make it true. If you say, "I am not a good teacher, so I'm not a part of the body," that doesn't make it true. If all of us were good at teaching, but none of us were good at hospitality, where would that leave us? (1 Corinthians 12:15-17).

This addresses a huge issue with comparison. The Bible goes to great pains, both here and other places, to express how God has made each of us unique, with differing skills, differing *levels* of skills, differing callings, and differing outcomes for faithful living.

Comparison only works if we're comparing two of the exact same thing. You can't compare apples to oranges, as they say. If we've decided that the characteristics of an orange are the best characteristics, then all the apples can ever do is fail. It will never be orange enough or tart enough. It will never tear into neat little sections no matter how hard it tries.

For many years, I felt like I didn't fit into the body of Christ because of my strong introversion. I wasn't antisocial, but I also wasn't good at all the extroverted activities I believed the church prioritized as good ministry and outreach. I always felt less-than because I'd decided (or internalized our society's implication that) extroversion was inherently better. I was an apple, and no matter how hard I tried, I couldn't turn myself into an orange.

But that's exactly what I did. I spent years trying to pretend to be an extrovert.

We could blame societal pressures for this, but ultimately, it was my own susceptibility to comparison.

I looked around and took note of who seemed to be most appreciated. Since those people were normally outgoing, talkative, and always in the middle of things, I tried to learn how to be outgoing, talkative, and always in the middle of things.

This just left me feeling exhausted and ineffective, because guess what? When you're faking, it feels fake—both to you and to those around you.

If the eye compares itself to the mouth and begins putting all its efforts into learning how to speak, it can only fail and feel even more inadequate.

We can all see how silly this is, can't we? The eye is not meant to speak, and if it spends all its time trying to learn to do so, it's also neglecting the job it *is* designed for. It leaves the body blind because it's not willing to play its role.

When we try to perform tasks that do not fit our giftings, it's not only discouraging for us, it takes away the task for someone who is qualified and leaves our own jobs undone.

When I began allowing myself to sit quietly while attending group events, gave myself the alone time I needed to process and write, and sought fellowship in smaller groups of two or three, I started to recognize that my gifts were, in fact, *gifts*.

God made me an introvert, but finding and understanding the strengths I had and how to incorporate them into the body of Christ was a long process.

I want to be clear that I don't mean none of us should ever step out side our comfort zones. I think many of us decide what our gifts are without ever consulting with the Lord, and sometimes, we don't know we have a gift until we try it. Additionally, sometimes God calls us to things that seem contrary to our gifts—like Moses being the liaison to Pharaoh when he could not speak well.

The bottom line is that we're always to let the Lord guide us into tasks rather than doing what we think looks best or what others pressure us into doing.

And let's talk about how my conclusions about value were based solely on external factors. I decided extroverts were more valuable because, from an observational standpoint, they get more attention. This makes us feel like they're more important.

But that's like saying that the hand is more important than the liver because everyone shakes it. It's not more important; it's just what's on the outside. It is *also* important, but the less visible parts of the body are not less important simply because they're not readily seen.

I should pause here to point out that I'm not degrading extroversion. Extroverts are also valuable; I'm only speaking from my own long years of believing they were *more* valuable.

I know it's also tempting to think, "Well, I'm a liver, and I guess that's okay, but I see lots of other livers livering better than I am."

The truth is that in the kingdom of God, no two of us are created exactly alike. The body of Christ is made of innumerable parts, and though some will have the same gifts, the expression and plans for those gifts are never exactly the same, nor are they given to the same degree.

In the Parable of the Talents, the master gives his servants tasks "each according to his own ability" (Matthew 25:15). Some are given more because they're capable of more, so measuring our results against others' is never valid.

The fact that some are capable of more is not a cause for jealousy, but a sobering truth. Luke 12:48 says, "From everyone who has been given much, much will be demanded; and to whom they entrusted much, of Him they will ask all the more."

Those who have great abilities or resources have a greater responsi-

## Taking Every Thought Captive

bility, and they will be judged accordingly. James 3:1 says, "Do not become teachers in large numbers, my brothers, since you know that we who are teachers will incur a stricter judgment."

At the same time, the Bible gives us many examples to show that those who have little can accomplish much. The Lord does not consider them "less-than" in the Kingdom of God.

The little boy gave his meager five loaves and two fish, and Jesus used it to feed a multitude (John 6:1-11). The little boy didn't have the skills nor the resources to cater such a feast, but the Lord used his obedience to create one.

The poor widow put her last two pennies into the offering box, and Jesus said, "Truly I say to you, this poor widow put in more than all the contributors to the treasury; for they all put in out of their surplus, but she, out of her poverty, put in all she owned, all she had to live on" (Mark 12:43-44).

He doesn't say she put in more *comparatively;* he literally says she put in more. God isn't concerned with abilities and resources we don't have; He's concerned with what we do with those abilities and resources we *do* have.

It boils down to this:

Do we believe it when He says He "arranged the parts, each one of them in the body, just as He desired" (1 Corinthians 12:18)?

Do we trust that we are truly "His workmanship, created in Christ Jesus for good works, which God prepared beforehand so that we would walk in them" (Ephesians 2:10)?

Or do we argue with Him and say, "What did You do? You made me wrong!" (Isaiah 45:9)?

Friends, we *can* trust Him. As our Maker, only He knows us intimately enough to know what He made us for and what He made us capable of. He knows us better than we know ourselves. He formed us exactly as we needed to be formed in order to accomplish the good works He prepared for us. He's given us everything we need for life and godliness through His power as God, and we have it through the true knowledge of Him (2 Peter 1:3).

# COMPARISON

Ponder this prayer from Psalm 139:

"You know when I sit down and when I get up; You understand my thought from far away. You scrutinize my path and my lying down and are acquainted with all my ways. Even before there is a word on my tongue, behold, Lord, You know it all. You have encircled me behind and in front and placed Your hand upon me. Such knowledge is too wonderful for me; it is too high, I cannot comprehend it. ... For You created my innermost parts; You wove me in my mother's womb. I will give thanks to You, because I am awesomely and wonderfully made; wonderful are Your works, and my soul knows it very well. My frame was not hidden from You when I was made in secret, and skillfully formed in the depths of the earth; Your eyes have seen my formless substance; and in Your book were written all the days that were ordained for me, when as yet there was not one of them. How precious also are Your thoughts for me, God! How vast is the sum of them! Were I to count them, they would outnumber the sand" (Psalm 139:1–6, 13–18).

Every one of us is awesomely and wonderfully made. Does your soul know it well?

Today I'm thankful for: _____
_____
_____

Anything about today that was:
True: _____
Honorable: _____
Pure: _____
Lovely: _____
Admirable: _____
Excellent: _____
Worthy of Praise: _____

A negative thought/lie I'm trying to retrain is: _____
_____
_____
_____

A Bible verse to teach myself the truth when that thought/lie arises is:
_____
_____
_____

A song, Bible verse, or quote I'm going to ponder throughout the day is:
_____
_____
_____

Successes, progress, or things I learned today: _____
_____
_____

A negative emotion I battled today was: _____

1. Was it appropriate to the situation*?   Yes ☐  No ☐
   (*Consider whether it was a real issue or influenced by mood, circumstance, or prior events.)
   - **If NO**, spend time in prayer and let it go, continually laying it at the feet of Jesus.
   - **If YES**, ask:
2. Is there anything productive* I can do about it?   Yes ☐  No ☐
   (*Consider whether it has potential to repair the issue & whether I will look back on the action with regret.)
   - **If NO**, spend time in prayer and let it go, continually laying it at the feet of Jesus.
   - **If YES**, ask:
3. What can I do, and how can I do it ASAP or implement a long-term plan? _____
   _____
   _____

4. Spend time in prayer and let it go, continually laying it at the feet of Jesus.

My prayer for the day: _____
_____
_____
_____

Random things I'd like to talk about, process, or remember: _____
_____
_____
_____

Today I'm thankful for: _____
_____
_____

Anything about today that was:
True: _____
Honorable: _____
Pure: _____
Lovely: _____
Admirable: _____
Excellent: _____
Worthy of Praise: _____

A negative thought/lie I'm trying to retrain is: _____
_____
_____
_____

A Bible verse to teach myself the truth when that thought/lie arises is:
_____
_____
_____

A song, Bible verse, or quote I'm going to ponder throughout the day is:
_____
_____
_____

Successes, progress, or things I learned today: _____
_____
_____

**A negative emotion I battled today was:** _____

1. Was it appropriate to the situation*?   Yes ☐  No ☐
   (*Consider whether it was a real issue or influenced by mood, circumstance, or prior events.)
   - **If NO**, spend time in prayer and let it go, continually laying it at the feet of Jesus.
   - **If YES**, ask:
2. Is there anything productive* I can do about it?   Yes ☐  No ☐
   (*Consider whether it has potential to repair the issue & whether I will look back on the action with regret.)
   - **If NO**, spend time in prayer and let it go, continually laying it at the feet of Jesus.
   - **If YES**, ask:
3. What can I do, and how can I do it ASAP or implement a long-term plan? _____
   _____
   _____

4. Spend time in prayer and let it go, continually laying it at the feet of Jesus.

**My prayer for the day:** _____
_____
_____
_____

**Random things I'd like to talk about, process, or remember:** _____
_____
_____
_____

Today I'm thankful for: _____
_____
_____

**Anything about today that was:**
True: _____
Honorable: _____
Pure: _____
Lovely: _____
Admirable: _____
Excellent: _____
Worthy of Praise: _____

A negative thought/lie I'm trying to retrain is: _____
_____
_____
_____

A Bible verse to teach myself the truth when that thought/lie arises is:
_____
_____
_____

A song, Bible verse, or quote I'm going to ponder throughout the day is:
_____
_____
_____

Successes, progress, or things I learned today: _____
_____
_____

**A negative emotion I battled today was:** _____

1. **Was it appropriate to the situation*?** Yes ☐ No ☐
   (*Consider whether it was a real issue or influenced by mood, circumstance, or prior events.)
   - **If NO**, spend time in prayer and let it go, continually laying it at the feet of Jesus.
   - **If YES**, ask:
2. **Is there anything productive* I can do about it?** Yes ☐ No ☐
   (*Consider whether it has potential to repair the issue & whether I will look back on the action with regret.)
   - **If NO**, spend time in prayer and let it go, continually laying it at the feet of Jesus.
   - **If YES**, ask:
3. **What can I do, and how can I do it ASAP or implement a long-term plan?** _____
   _____
   _____

4. **Spend time in prayer and let it go, continually laying it at the feet of Jesus.**

**My prayer for the day:** _____
_____
_____
_____

**Random things I'd like to talk about, process, or remember:** _____
_____
_____

Today I'm thankful for: _____
_____
_____

Anything about today that was:
True: _____
Honorable: _____
Pure: _____
Lovely: _____
Admirable: _____
Excellent: _____
Worthy of Praise: _____

A negative thought/lie I'm trying to retrain is: _____
_____
_____
_____

A Bible verse to teach myself the truth when that thought/lie arises is:
_____
_____
_____

A song, Bible verse, or quote I'm going to ponder throughout the day is:
_____
_____
_____

Successes, progress, or things I learned today: _____
_____
_____

A negative emotion I battled today was: _____

1. Was it appropriate to the situation*?   Yes ☐  No ☐
   (*Consider whether it was a real issue or influenced by mood, circumstance, or prior events.)
   - **If NO**, spend time in prayer and let it go, continually laying it at the feet of Jesus.
   - **If YES**, ask:
2. Is there anything productive* I can do about it?   Yes ☐  No ☐
   (*Consider whether it has potential to repair the issue & whether I will look back on the action with regret.)
   - **If NO**, spend time in prayer and let it go, continually laying it at the feet of Jesus.
   - **If YES**, ask:
3. What can I do, and how can I do it ASAP or implement a long-term plan? _____
   _____
   _____

4. Spend time in prayer and let it go, continually laying it at the feet of Jesus.

My prayer for the day: _____
_____
_____
_____

Random things I'd like to talk about, process, or remember: _____
_____
_____
_____

Today I'm thankful for: _____

_____

_____

**Anything about today that was:**

True: _____

Honorable: _____

Pure: _____

Lovely: _____

Admirable: _____

Excellent: _____

Worthy of Praise: _____

A negative thought/lie I'm trying to retrain is: _____

_____

_____

_____

A Bible verse to teach myself the truth when that thought/lie arises is:

_____

_____

_____

A song, Bible verse, or quote I'm going to ponder throughout the day is:

_____

_____

_____

Successes, progress, or things I learned today: _____

_____

_____

**A negative emotion I battled today was:** _____

1. **Was it appropriate to the situation*?** Yes ☐ No ☐
   (*Consider whether it was a real issue or influenced by mood, circumstance, or prior events.)
   - **If NO**, spend time in prayer and let it go, continually laying it at the feet of Jesus.
   - **If YES**, ask:
2. **Is there anything productive* I can do about it?** Yes ☐ No ☐
   (*Consider whether it has potential to repair the issue & whether I will look back on the action with regret.)
   - **If NO**, spend time in prayer and let it go, continually laying it at the feet of Jesus.
   - **If YES**, ask:
3. What can I do, and how can I do it ASAP or implement a long-term plan? _____
   _____
   _____

4. Spend time in prayer and let it go, continually laying it at the feet of Jesus.

**My prayer for the day:** _____
_____
_____
_____

**Random things I'd like to talk about, process, or remember:** _____
_____
_____
_____

Today I'm thankful for: _____
_____
_____

**Anything about today that was:**
True: _____
Honorable: _____
Pure: _____
Lovely: _____
Admirable: _____
Excellent: _____
Worthy of Praise: _____

A negative thought/lie I'm trying to retrain is: _____
_____
_____
_____

A Bible verse to teach myself the truth when that thought/lie arises is:
_____
_____
_____

A song, Bible verse, or quote I'm going to ponder throughout the day is:
_____
_____
_____

Successes, progress, or things I learned today: _____
_____
_____

A negative emotion I battled today was: _____

1. Was it appropriate to the situation*?   Yes ☐  No ☐
   (*Consider whether it was a real issue or influenced by mood, circumstance, or prior events.)
   - If **NO**, spend time in prayer and let it go, continually laying it at the feet of Jesus.
   - If **YES**, ask:
2. Is there anything productive* I can do about it?   Yes ☐  No ☐
   (*Consider whether it has potential to repair the issue & whether I will look back on the action with regret.)
   - If **NO**, spend time in prayer and let it go, continually laying it at the feet of Jesus.
   - If **YES**, ask:
3. What can I do, and how can I do it ASAP or implement a long-term plan? _____
   _____
   _____

4. Spend time in prayer and let it go, continually laying it at the feet of Jesus.

My prayer for the day: _____
_____
_____
_____

Random things I'd like to talk about, process, or remember: _____
_____
_____
_____

Today I'm thankful for: _____
_____
_____

**Anything about today that was:**
True: _____
Honorable: _____
Pure: _____
Lovely: _____
Admirable: _____
Excellent: _____
Worthy of Praise: _____

A negative thought/lie I'm trying to retrain is: _____
_____
_____
_____

A Bible verse to teach myself the truth when that thought/lie arises is:
_____
_____
_____

A song, Bible verse, or quote I'm going to ponder throughout the day is:
_____
_____
_____

Successes, progress, or things I learned today: _____
_____
_____

**A negative emotion I battled today was:** _____

1. **Was it appropriate to the situation\*?**   Yes ☐   No ☐
   (*Consider whether it was a real issue or influenced by mood, circumstance, or prior events.)
   - **If NO**, spend time in prayer and let it go, continually laying it at the feet of Jesus.
   - **If YES**, ask:

2. **Is there anything productive\* I can do about it?**   Yes ☐   No ☐
   (*Consider whether it has potential to repair the issue & whether I will look back on the action with regret.)
   - **If NO**, spend time in prayer and let it go, continually laying it at the feet of Jesus.
   - **If YES**, ask:

3. **What can I do, and how can I do it ASAP or implement a long-term plan?** _____
   _____
   _____

4. Spend time in prayer and let it go, continually laying it at the feet of Jesus.

**My prayer for the day:** _____
_____
_____
_____

**Random things I'd like to talk about, process, or remember:** _____
_____
_____
_____

# Notes

# Wrong Metrics

Another huge issue with comparison is that the standards we use are almost always based on worldly metrics. There's no human way to value a person's contribution to the Kingdom of God.

You can't chart effectiveness in prayer, quantify love for God and others, or keep statistics on encouraging other believers.

We've already seen that Jesus prized the widow's last two pennies over what others gave out of their excess. From a worldly perspective, no one would ever say she gave "more" (Luke 21:1-4).

1 Samuel 16:7 says, "For the Lord sees not as man sees; for man looks at the outward appearance, but the Lord looks at the heart."

None of us can see anyone else's heart, and we can't even see our own clearly.

We're not capable of determining who is the greatest or the least. And even if we could, we shouldn't. Because hierarchy isn't what the Kingdom of God is about—or rather, if there is a hierarchy, it's reversed.

Let's look at a few examples.

Matthew 20:16 says the last shall be first.

Luke 14:7-11 tells us never to seek the places of honor, for "everyone who exalts himself will be humbled, and the one who humbles himself will be exalted."

When James and John wanted proof they were doing better than the other disciples, they were reprimanded. Jesus reminded them that even He didn't come to be honored, but to be a servant. He told them if they wanted to be first, they had to follow His example and be willing to be slaves (Matthew 20:20-28, Mark 10:35-45).

When the disciples argued over who was greatest, they were scolded

## Taking Every Thought Captive

(Luke 9:46-48). Jesus reminded them that we all must come into the Kingdom of God as humble as little children, utterly dependent, unable to make our own way, and subject to authority (Matthew 18:1-4).

It's clear that, according to Jesus, our ideas of greatness need to drastically change.

But let's also talk about what comparison looks like practically.

Comparison is basing our worth on how we measure up to other people. If we see others doing better than us, we feel bad. If we see others doing worse than us, we feel good.

I know, I know. That's not how we'd put it.

But we need to face the fact that when comparison has the power to make us feel good or bad, then feeling good implicitly means that we're glad others are doing worse than us. It may not require that *everyone* is doing worse than us, but usually a firm majority.

A few years ago, the Lord strongly convicted me about this. We often trick ourselves into thinking it's okay since this comparison generally makes us feel worse in a society where we can constantly compare ourselves to the best of the best. We think, "Of course comparison would be bad if it made us prideful and arrogant!" But since it makes us feel bad about ourselves, we look for pity rather than correction.

The truth is there's simply no place in Christianity for a satisfaction with life and myself dependent on whether I'm doing better than others. It makes us rivals, not supporters. If we allow it to reign in our lives, then even when we want to be happy for others, we struggle. It's always harmful.

If I see someone I used to know who's gained more weight than I have and feel even the slightest tinge of relief because it makes me feel better about myself, that's not okay.

If I look around at book reviews and feel a little confidence boost to find that mine are stronger than someone else's, that's not okay. (I'm gettin' real personal now, y'all!)

If we're looking around at others and feeling better about ourselves, we're almost always feeling good about something that person likely struggles with—something that makes *them* feel insecure—and that's not okay.

## Wrong Metrics

There's nothing wrong with wanting to do things well or wanting our lives to go well; that's not the problem. The harm comes from believing how well or badly we're doing is determined by measuring against others' achievements. If that's our standard, then we can't wish we were doing better without wishing others were doing worse.

When we live by comparison, we can't win unless someone else is losing.

We do this frequently in so many areas—looks, talent, relationships, finances, possessions, popularity, or success. It's never okay.

Philippians 2:3-4 says, "Do nothing from selfishness or empty conceit, but with humility consider one another as more important than yourselves; do not merely look out for your own personal interests, but also for the interests of others."

It's never considering others more important than myself or looking out for their interests if I find it difficult to even be happy for their successes and blessings because it makes me feel bad about myself.

That passage goes on to talk about how Jesus—who deserved every knee to bow to Him—lowered himself to the place of a servant. This attitude isn't about pretending or thinking we don't deserve anything good; it's about not caring if we get it, whether we deserve it or not, because we've set our mind on things above (Colossians 3:2).

And there's another way in which comparison can harm. When we struggle, we often look around at others and wonder why they don't have it as bad as we do. If we ruminate on that, we'll become bitter and resent the path God has for us.

In John 21:18-23, Jesus told Peter that he was going to be martyred, and Peter's immediate reaction was to compare. He turned around, pointed at John and asked, "What about him?"

Jesus's answer essentially amounted to, "That's none of your business. You follow Me."

What someone else's path looks like has no bearing on what we're supposed to do—we're to follow Jesus no matter what.

In the end, if we continue to believe that our worth and the value of our lives is bound up in those worldly metrics like looks, talent, relationships, finances, possessions, popularity, success, or accomplishment, it's going to be hard for us to get over comparison.

That's why I wrote the section on living our purpose first—to show that our true purpose has nothing to do with any of those things.

When we truly know and believe that purpose is about loving God, following His commandments, living justly, showing mercy, walking humbly with God, showing compassion to those who need help, serving others, and living out the fruit of the Spirit, there's *nothing to compare.*

We can all be winners. Others' successes don't threaten our self-esteem when it's bound up in Christ instead of the things of this world. To lose our life really is to find it, and not only in an eternal sense (Matthew 16:25).

How freeing it is to not be held captive by comparison and to stop the never-ending, ever-changing scramble to meet the world's standards!

We can never stay young enough, fashionable enough, rich enough, smart enough, capable enough, healthy enough, or strong enough to stay in the world's good graces. And even if we do, we often become an object of jealousy rather than love, have squandered resources irresponsibly to get there, and will be behind again next year unless we persist in the rat race.

Eventually, no matter what we do and even if nothing else fails us, our bodies will decline. If we've placed our hope in the world's approval, we will despair as we become more unnoticed, undervalued, and unable.

We can rush around trying to meet all these expectations for as long as our circumstances allow, or we can begin to trust that our worth is based on God's standards now—standards that are achievable by everyone at every stage of life.

As Paul says, "For am I now seeking the favor of people, or of God? Or am I striving to please people? If I were still trying to please people, I would not be a bondservant of Christ" (Galatians 1:10).

We're no longer captive to seeking approval from man, who cannot see the heart nor measure by eternal value.

We can live the truth that Jeremiah 9:23–24 speaks: "'Let no wise man boast of his wisdom, nor let the mighty man boast of his might,

## Wrong Metrics

nor a rich man boast of his riches; but let the one who boasts boast of this, that he understands and knows Me, that I am the Lord who exercises mercy, justice, and righteousness on the earth; for I delight in these things,' declares the Lord."

May it be the goal of every believer never to boast in wisdom, might, riches, or any other earthly advantage, but only to boast in understanding and knowing our God!

Our worldly comparison bears no good fruit. It will always only lead us to pride and looking down on others, insecurity that keeps us from investing the talents God has given us, or bitterness and jealousy that we're not getting what we deserve when others are. It keeps us focused on ourselves in the worst ways rather than focused on Christ or on loving others.

There's only one place the Bible ever speaks positively of comparison—that's by "outdoing one another in showing honor" (Romans 12:10). Some versions say by "giving preference to one another in honor."

How lovely our world and how appealing the church would be if we followed this teaching and our only attempts at competition were to see who could honor the other person more?

If we must compete, may this be our only criteria for winning!

**Today I'm thankful for:** _____
_____
_____

**Anything about today that was:**
True: _____
Honorable: _____
Pure: _____
Lovely: _____
Admirable: _____
Excellent: _____
Worthy of Praise: _____

**A negative thought/lie I'm trying to retrain is:** _____
_____
_____
_____

**A Bible verse to teach myself the truth when that thought/lie arises is:**
_____
_____
_____

**A song, Bible verse, or quote I'm going to ponder throughout the day is:**
_____
_____
_____

**Successes, progress, or things I learned today:** _____
_____
_____

**A negative emotion I battled today was:** _____

1. **Was it appropriate to the situation*?**  Yes ☐  No ☐
   (*Consider whether it was a real issue or influenced by mood, circumstance, or prior events.)
   - **If NO**, spend time in prayer and let it go, continually laying it at the feet of Jesus.
   - **If YES**, ask:
2. **Is there anything productive* I can do about it?**  Yes ☐  No ☐
   (*Consider whether it has potential to repair the issue & whether I will look back on the action with regret.)
   - **If NO**, spend time in prayer and let it go, continually laying it at the feet of Jesus.
   - **If YES**, ask:
3. **What can I do, and how can I do it ASAP or implement a long-term plan?** _____
   _____
   _____

4. **Spend time in prayer and let it go, continually laying it at the feet of Jesus.**

**My prayer for the day:** _____
_____
_____
_____

**Random things I'd like to talk about, process, or remember:** _____
_____
_____
_____

Today I'm thankful for: _____
_____
_____

**Anything about today that was:**
True: _____
Honorable: _____
Pure: _____
Lovely: _____
Admirable: _____
Excellent: _____
Worthy of Praise: _____

A negative thought/lie I'm trying to retrain is: _____
_____
_____
_____

A Bible verse to teach myself the truth when that thought/lie arises is:
_____
_____
_____

A song, Bible verse, or quote I'm going to ponder throughout the day is:
_____
_____
_____

Successes, progress, or things I learned today: _____
_____
_____

**A negative emotion I battled today was:** _____

1. **Was it appropriate to the situation*?**   Yes ☐  No ☐
   (*Consider whether it was a real issue or influenced by mood, circumstance, or prior events.)
   - **If NO**, spend time in prayer and let it go, continually laying it at the feet of Jesus.
   - **If YES**, ask:
2. **Is there anything productive* I can do about it?**   Yes ☐  No ☐
   (*Consider whether it has potential to repair the issue & whether I will look back on the action with regret.)
   - **If NO**, spend time in prayer and let it go, continually laying it at the feet of Jesus.
   - **If YES**, ask:
3. **What can I do, and how can I do it ASAP or implement a long-term plan?** _____
   _____
   _____

4. **Spend time in prayer and let it go, continually laying it at the feet of Jesus.**

**My prayer for the day:** _____
_____
_____
_____

**Random things I'd like to talk about, process, or remember:** _____
_____
_____
_____

Today I'm thankful for: _____

_____

_____

**Anything about today that was:**
True: _____
Honorable: _____
Pure: _____
Lovely: _____
Admirable: _____
Excellent: _____
Worthy of Praise: _____

A negative thought/lie I'm trying to retrain is: _____

_____

_____

_____

A Bible verse to teach myself the truth when that thought/lie arises is:

_____

_____

_____

A song, Bible verse, or quote I'm going to ponder throughout the day is:

_____

_____

_____

Successes, progress, or things I learned today: _____

_____

_____

A negative emotion I battled today was: _____

1. Was it appropriate to the situation*?  Yes ☐  No ☐
   (*Consider whether it was a real issue or influenced by mood, circumstance, or prior events.)
   - If **NO**, spend time in prayer and let it go, continually laying it at the feet of Jesus.
   - If **YES**, ask:
2. Is there anything productive* I can do about it?  Yes ☐  No ☐
   (*Consider whether it has potential to repair the issue & whether I will look back on the action with regret.)
   - If **NO**, spend time in prayer and let it go, continually laying it at the feet of Jesus.
   - If **YES**, ask:
3. What can I do, and how can I do it ASAP or implement a long-term plan? _____
   _____
   _____

4. Spend time in prayer and let it go, continually laying it at the feet of Jesus.

My prayer for the day: _____
_____
_____
_____

Random things I'd like to talk about, process, or remember: _____
_____
_____

Today I'm thankful for: _____
_____
_____

**Anything about today that was:**
True: _____
Honorable: _____
Pure: _____
Lovely: _____
Admirable: _____
Excellent: _____
Worthy of Praise: _____

A negative thought/lie I'm trying to retrain is: _____
_____
_____
_____

A Bible verse to teach myself the truth when that thought/lie arises is:
_____
_____
_____

A song, Bible verse, or quote I'm going to ponder throughout the day is:
_____
_____
_____

Successes, progress, or things I learned today: _____
_____
_____

**A negative emotion I battled today was:** _____

1. **Was it appropriate to the situation*?**   Yes ☐  No ☐
   (*Consider whether it was a real issue or influenced by mood, circumstance, or prior events.)
   - **If NO**, spend time in prayer and let it go, continually laying it at the feet of Jesus.
   - **If YES**, ask:
2. **Is there anything productive* I can do about it?**  Yes ☐  No ☐
   (*Consider whether it has potential to repair the issue & whether I will look back on the action with regret.)
   - **If NO**, spend time in prayer and let it go, continually laying it at the feet of Jesus.
   - **If YES**, ask:
3. **What can I do, and how can I do it ASAP or implement a long-term plan?** _____
   _____
   _____

4. **Spend time in prayer and let it go, continually laying it at the feet of Jesus.**

**My prayer for the day:** _____
_____
_____
_____

**Random things I'd like to talk about, process, or remember:** _____
_____
_____
_____

Today I'm thankful for: _____
_____
_____

Anything about today that was:
True: _____
Honorable: _____
Pure: _____
Lovely: _____
Admirable: _____
Excellent: _____
Worthy of Praise: _____

A negative thought/lie I'm trying to retrain is: _____
_____
_____
_____

A Bible verse to teach myself the truth when that thought/lie arises is:
_____
_____
_____

A song, Bible verse, or quote I'm going to ponder throughout the day is:
_____
_____
_____

Successes, progress, or things I learned today: _____
_____
_____

**A negative emotion I battled today was:** _____

1. **Was it appropriate to the situation*?**  Yes ☐  No ☐
   (*Consider whether it was a real issue or influenced by mood, circumstance, or prior events.)
   - **If NO**, spend time in prayer and let it go, continually laying it at the feet of Jesus.
   - **If YES**, ask:
2. **Is there anything productive* I can do about it?**  Yes ☐  No ☐
   (*Consider whether it has potential to repair the issue & whether I will look back on the action with regret.)
   - **If NO**, spend time in prayer and let it go, continually laying it at the feet of Jesus.
   - **If YES**, ask:
3. **What can I do, and how can I do it ASAP or implement a long-term plan?** _____
   _____
   _____

4. **Spend time in prayer and let it go, continually laying it at the feet of Jesus.**

**My prayer for the day:** _____
_____
_____
_____

**Random things I'd like to talk about, process, or remember:** _____
_____
_____
_____

Today I'm thankful for: _____
_____
_____

Anything about today that was:
True: _____
Honorable: _____
Pure: _____
Lovely: _____
Admirable: _____
Excellent: _____
Worthy of Praise: _____

A negative thought/lie I'm trying to retrain is: _____
_____
_____
_____

A Bible verse to teach myself the truth when that thought/lie arises is:
_____
_____
_____

A song, Bible verse, or quote I'm going to ponder throughout the day is:
_____
_____
_____

Successes, progress, or things I learned today: _____
_____
_____

A negative emotion I battled today was: _____

1. **Was it appropriate to the situation\*?**   Yes ☐  No ☐
   (\*Consider whether it was a real issue or influenced by mood, circumstance, or prior events.)
   - **If NO**, spend time in prayer and let it go, continually laying it at the feet of Jesus.
   - **If YES**, ask:
2. **Is there anything productive\* I can do about it?**   Yes ☐  No ☐
   (\*Consider whether it has potential to repair the issue & whether I will look back on the action with regret.)
   - **If NO**, spend time in prayer and let it go, continually laying it at the feet of Jesus.
   - **If YES**, ask:
3. What can I do, and how can I do it ASAP or implement a long-term plan? _____
   _____
   _____

4. Spend time in prayer and let it go, continually laying it at the feet of Jesus.

My prayer for the day: _____
_____
_____
_____

Random things I'd like to talk about, process, or remember: _____
_____
_____
_____

Today I'm thankful for: _____
_____
_____

Anything about today that was:
True: _____
Honorable: _____
Pure: _____
Lovely: _____
Admirable: _____
Excellent: _____
Worthy of Praise: _____

A negative thought/lie I'm trying to retrain is: _____
_____
_____
_____

A Bible verse to teach myself the truth when that thought/lie arises is:
_____
_____
_____

A song, Bible verse, or quote I'm going to ponder throughout the day is:
_____
_____
_____

Successes, progress, or things I learned today: _____
_____
_____

A negative emotion I battled today was: _____

1. Was it appropriate to the situation*?   Yes ☐  No ☐
   (*Consider whether it was a real issue or influenced by mood, circumstance, or prior events.)
   - **If NO**, spend time in prayer and let it go, continually laying it at the feet of Jesus.
   - **If YES**, ask:
2. Is there anything productive* I can do about it?  Yes ☐  No ☐
   (*Consider whether it has potential to repair the issue & whether I will look back on the action with regret.)
   - **If NO**, spend time in prayer and let it go, continually laying it at the feet of Jesus.
   - **If YES**, ask:
3. What can I do, and how can I do it ASAP or implement a long-term plan? _____
   _____
   _____

4. Spend time in prayer and let it go, continually laying it at the feet of Jesus.

My prayer for the day: _____
_____
_____
_____

Random things I'd like to talk about, process, or remember: _____
_____
_____
_____

# Notes

# Obedience Is Freedom

I recently realized that every time I pondered obedience, an image popped into my head along with it.

It's like in those old allergy medication commercials where someone is trudging along in a dreary, black-and-white world, sniffling and sneezing. Then they take the medicine, and in a flash, everything around them bursts into vibrant color! They're suddenly laughing with friends and frolicking through fields of flowers.

They've been freed from the misery of something that tainted everything in their lives before.

That's what obedience does for us. It allows us to revel in all the beauty God intended for us to enjoy, free from the snares and misery of the sins that once held us captive (Romans 6:5–14).

Psalm 119:45 says, "I will walk at liberty, for I seek Your precepts," and it's so true.

Obedience sets us free, but I know that's not how most of us see it. We see it as restrictive—something keeping us from doing what we want.

That's how it feels at first, like you're climbing up an impossibly steep hill, like no one could keep up this much effort, and like there's no end in sight.

That's not foreign to me; it's how I saw it for years, and I'd be lying if I said I didn't still have moments I see it that way.

But that feeling is a lie.

We can't see the top of the hill, but it's there, and when we reach it, the road levels out. What had been an arduous journey becomes a pleasant walk.

## Taking Every Thought Captive

We all understand "no pain, no gain" as it applies to physical health, exercise, and strength, but no one tells us the same is true of spiritual health. It's always going to be harder until we've built up spiritual endurance and muscle.

Most of us hit the point where the climb toward obedience begins to feel impossibly hard, and we turn around. We can't see that the top of the hill is just ahead, so we take a few steps back down. We give in to the temptation and let the Enemy take a little ground back. We don't intend to quit; we just want to relax for a minute. But by doing this over and over and over, we make our journey longer than it has to be, and we wear ourselves out.

That's when the devil comes for us. Just like the roaring lion, he seeks to devour the weak and exhausted (1 Peter 5:8).

How many times do we turn around just before we reach the top because we think we don't have what we need to overcome?

But Jesus says, "My food is to do the will of Him who sent Me, and to accomplish His work." Doing God's will is the food we need; only that will supply the energy we need to keep climbing. It's our spiritual sustenance.

Turning back to sin will never give us the fuel we need to obey; it will always set us back, just like junk food will always impede rather than enable us to build muscle.

So how do we do begin this journey uphill?

Jesus said that "everyone who commits sin is a slave of sin" (John 8:34), so part of being freed is acting on the things the Bible tells us to do—to "flee from [sin] and pursue righteousness" (1 Timothy 6:11, 2 Timothy 2:22).

James 4:7-8 says, "Submit therefore to God. But resist the devil, and he will flee from you. Come close to God and He will come close to you. Cleanse your hands, you sinners; and purify your hearts."

Romans 8:13-14 says, "For if you are living in accord with the flesh, you are going to die; but if by the Spirit you are putting to death the deeds of the body, you will live. For all who are being led by the Spirit of God, these are sons and daughters of God."

## Obedience Is Freedom

Romans 12:1 says, "Present your bodies as a living and holy sacrifice, acceptable to God, which is your spiritual service of worship."

All these words are active—submit, resist, cleanse, purify, put to death, flee, pursue, present your bodies. It says this is how we worship. It isn't easy; we're fighting a battle between our flesh and the Spirit of God within us (Galatians 5:16-24).

But we're not powerless. These are all things that we can do—that indeed we're instructed to do.

Discipline is essential if we're going to become spiritually healthy just like it's necessary to become physically healthy. Every step taken up the hill builds the Spirit's power in us and weakens the hold our flesh has over us.

Philippians 2:13 says, "for it is God who works in you, both to will and to work for his good pleasure."

The Holy Spirit gives us the power not only to *will* God's good pleasure, but also to *work* at doing it. He doesn't stop at giving us the desire to follow Him; He gives us what we need in order to actually follow.

In her book *Discipline*, Elisabeth Elliot says, "Choices will continually be necessary, and let us not forget—POSSIBLE. Obedience to God is always possible. It is a deadly error to fall into the notion that when feelings are extremely strong, we can do nothing but act on them."

God always gives us a way to escape temptation (1 Corinthians 10:13).

From the outside, obedience looks like confinement, but for any *Doctor Who* fans—believe me when I tell you that obedience is *bigger on the inside*. Through it, the Lord "brought me out into an open place" (Psalm 18:19), and now I can "walk in liberty" (Psalm 119:45).

I can say this a hundred times in a hundred different ways, but it's hard to believe until you experience it.

John 7:17 says, "If anyone is willing to do His will, he will know about the teaching." Some things we simply can't understand until we obey; we won't begin to *know* until after we do.

To sum it up with another quote from Elisabeth Elliot's book, *Discipline*, "Try it. When, in the face of powerful temptation to do wrong, there is the swift, hard renunciation, 'I will not,' it will be followed by the sudden loosing of the bonds of self, the yes to God that lets in sunlight, sets us singing, and all freedom's bells clanging for joy."

If you've never tasted this kind of freedom, *fight for it* (1 Timothy 6:12). Walk up that hill, and don't turn around. "It was for freedom that Christ set us free," so let's not fall into slavery to sin once more (Galatians 5:1).

Without obedience, we'll always be like those people in the allergy commercials walking around in black and white before the medicine kicks in, unable to enjoy the beauty around us and never truly experiencing the fullness of relationship with God.

I'm not saying that obedience will turn the events of your life into a perpetual fairy tale. The circumstances around you may still be difficult. The freedom you gain is internal, but that doesn't make it less valuable. Hard things will happen in our lives no matter what; living like this gives us the power to walk through them with courage, strength, and confidence in God's purpose.

And none of this means I'm perfect. I still sin (1 John 1:8), but there are no Enemy strongholds left in my life. I've opened all the dark, shuttered places up to God and submitted them to Him. I no longer clench my fists before Him, unwilling to let go of the trash I've picked up in the world, thinking it's treasure.

I also want to draw a distinction between the kind of obedience the Pharisees walked vs. obedience walked in love. Most of us can see that godly obedience will not lead to pride, preferential treatment, oppression, looking down on others, or ignoring people's needs, but it also shouldn't lead to despair or hopelessness at failures. (See the section on regret!) If it looks like one of these things, then either our hearts and motives are being influenced by the Enemy, or our view of the Lord is still skewed.

The Bible says, "If you love Me, you will keep My commandments" (John 14:15), and that "We love, because He first loved us" (1 John 4:19). If we follow this motivation backwards, we must 1) know that He loves us, 2) so we can love Him, and 3) our love will lead to our obedience.

If we don't know that God truly loves us, our obedience will always feel like wary white-knuckling subjection to a distant, dubious

## Obedience Is Freedom

authority rather than trusting our loving Father to guide us into something beautiful.

Now, because I see and have experienced the greatness of His love for me, when He prompts me to change my attitude, asks me to give something up, or tells me to do something my flesh doesn't readily want to, I *believe* the truth that "His commandments are not burdensome" (1 John 5:3). Believing this truth makes obedience easier and easier each time.

This is my prayer for you—that you will try it and learn for yourself that His commandments are not burdensome!

"Blessed are those who hear the word of God and follow it" (Luke 11:28)!

Today I'm thankful for: _____
_____
_____

**Anything about today that was:**
True: _____
Honorable: _____
Pure: _____
Lovely: _____
Admirable: _____
Excellent: _____
Worthy of Praise: _____

A negative thought/lie I'm trying to retrain is: _____
_____
_____
_____

A Bible verse to teach myself the truth when that thought/lie arises is:
_____
_____
_____

A song, Bible verse, or quote I'm going to ponder throughout the day is:
_____
_____
_____

Successes, progress, or things I learned today: _____
_____
_____

**A negative emotion I battled today was:** _____

1. **Was it appropriate to the situation*?**   Yes ☐  No ☐
   (*Consider whether it was a real issue or influenced by mood, circumstance, or prior events.)
   - **If NO**, spend time in prayer and let it go, continually laying it at the feet of Jesus.
   - **If YES**, ask:
2. **Is there anything productive* I can do about it?**   Yes ☐  No ☐
   (*Consider whether it has potential to repair the issue & whether I will look back on the action with regret.)
   - **If NO**, spend time in prayer and let it go, continually laying it at the feet of Jesus.
   - **If YES**, ask:
3. **What can I do, and how can I do it ASAP or implement a long-term plan?** _____
   _____
   _____

4. **Spend time in prayer and let it go, continually laying it at the feet of Jesus.**

**My prayer for the day:** _____
_____
_____
_____

**Random things I'd like to talk about, process, or remember:** _____
_____
_____
_____

Today I'm thankful for: _____
_____
_____

Anything about today that was:
True: _____
Honorable: _____
Pure: _____
Lovely: _____
Admirable: _____
Excellent: _____
Worthy of Praise: _____

A negative thought/lie I'm trying to retrain is: _____
_____
_____
_____

A Bible verse to teach myself the truth when that thought/lie arises is:
_____
_____
_____

A song, Bible verse, or quote I'm going to ponder throughout the day is:
_____
_____
_____

Successes, progress, or things I learned today: _____
_____
_____

**A negative emotion I battled today was:** _____

1. **Was it appropriate to the situation*?**  Yes ☐  No ☐
   (*Consider whether it was a real issue or influenced by mood, circumstance, or prior events.)
   - **If NO**, spend time in prayer and let it go, continually laying it at the feet of Jesus.
   - **If YES**, ask:

2. **Is there anything productive* I can do about it?**  Yes ☐  No ☐
   (*Consider whether it has potential to repair the issue & whether I will look back on the action with regret.)
   - **If NO**, spend time in prayer and let it go, continually laying it at the feet of Jesus.
   - **If YES**, ask:

3. **What can I do, and how can I do it ASAP or implement a long-term plan?** _____
   _____
   _____

4. **Spend time in prayer and let it go, continually laying it at the feet of Jesus.**

**My prayer for the day:** _____
_____
_____
_____

**Random things I'd like to talk about, process, or remember:** _____
_____
_____
_____

Today I'm thankful for:

Anything about today that was:
True:
Honorable:
Pure:
Lovely:
Admirable:
Excellent:
Worthy of Praise:

A negative thought/lie I'm trying to retrain is:

A Bible verse to teach myself the truth when that thought/lie arises is:

A song, Bible verse, or quote I'm going to ponder throughout the day is:

Successes, progress, or things I learned today:

**A negative emotion I battled today was:** _____

1. **Was it appropriate to the situation\*?**   Yes ☐  No ☐
   (\*Consider whether it was a real issue or influenced by mood, circumstance, or prior events.)
   - **If NO**, spend time in prayer and let it go, continually laying it at the feet of Jesus.
   - **If YES**, ask:
2. **Is there anything productive\* I can do about it?**  Yes ☐  No ☐
   (\*Consider whether it has potential to repair the issue & whether I will look back on the action with regret.)
   - **If NO**, spend time in prayer and let it go, continually laying it at the feet of Jesus.
   - **If YES**, ask:
3. What can I do, and how can I do it ASAP or implement a long-term plan?_____

   _____

   _____

4. Spend time in prayer and let it go, continually laying it at the feet of Jesus.

**My prayer for the day:** _____

_____

_____

_____

**Random things I'd like to talk about, process, or remember:** _____

_____

_____

_____

Today I'm thankful for: _____
_____
_____

Anything about today that was:
True: _____
Honorable: _____
Pure: _____
Lovely: _____
Admirable: _____
Excellent: _____
Worthy of Praise: _____

A negative thought/lie I'm trying to retrain is: _____
_____
_____
_____

A Bible verse to teach myself the truth when that thought/lie arises is:
_____
_____
_____

A song, Bible verse, or quote I'm going to ponder throughout the day is:
_____
_____
_____

Successes, progress, or things I learned today: _____
_____
_____

**A negative emotion I battled today was:** _____

1. **Was it appropriate to the situation*?**  Yes ☐  No ☐
   (*Consider whether it was a real issue or influenced by mood, circumstance, or prior events.)
   - **If NO**, spend time in prayer and let it go, continually laying it at the feet of Jesus.
   - **If YES**, ask:
2. **Is there anything productive* I can do about it?**  Yes ☐  No ☐
   (*Consider whether it has potential to repair the issue & whether I will look back on the action with regret.)
   - **If NO**, spend time in prayer and let it go, continually laying it at the feet of Jesus.
   - **If YES**, ask:
3. What can I do, and how can I do it ASAP or implement a long-term plan? _____
   _____
   _____

4. Spend time in prayer and let it go, continually laying it at the feet of Jesus.

**My prayer for the day:** _____
_____
_____
_____

**Random things I'd like to talk about, process, or remember:** _____
_____
_____
_____

Today I'm thankful for: _____
_____
_____

**Anything about today that was:**
True: _____
Honorable: _____
Pure: _____
Lovely: _____
Admirable: _____
Excellent: _____
Worthy of Praise: _____

A negative thought/lie I'm trying to retrain is: _____
_____
_____
_____

A Bible verse to teach myself the truth when that thought/lie arises is:
_____
_____
_____

A song, Bible verse, or quote I'm going to ponder throughout the day is:
_____
_____
_____

Successes, progress, or things I learned today: _____
_____
_____

A negative emotion I battled today was: _____

1. Was it appropriate to the situation*?   Yes ☐ No ☐
   (*Consider whether it was a real issue or influenced by mood, circumstance, or prior events.)
   - **If NO**, spend time in prayer and let it go, continually laying it at the feet of Jesus.
   - **If YES**, ask:
2. Is there anything productive* I can do about it?  Yes ☐ No ☐
   (*Consider whether it has potential to repair the issue & whether I will look back on the action with regret.)
   - **If NO**, spend time in prayer and let it go, continually laying it at the feet of Jesus.
   - **If YES**, ask:
3. What can I do, and how can I do it ASAP or implement a long-term plan?_____

4. Spend time in prayer and let it go, continually laying it at the feet of Jesus.

My prayer for the day: _____

Random things I'd like to talk about, process, or remember: _____

**Today I'm thankful for:** _____
_____
_____

**Anything about today that was:**
True: _____
Honorable: _____
Pure: _____
Lovely: _____
Admirable: _____
Excellent: _____
Worthy of Praise: _____

**A negative thought/lie I'm trying to retrain is:** _____
_____
_____
_____

**A Bible verse to teach myself the truth when that thought/lie arises is:**
_____
_____
_____

**A song, Bible verse, or quote I'm going to ponder throughout the day is:**
_____
_____
_____

**Successes, progress, or things I learned today:** _____
_____
_____

A negative emotion I battled today was: _____

1. Was it appropriate to the situation*?   Yes ☐   No ☐
   (*Consider whether it was a real issue or influenced by mood, circumstance, or prior events.)
   - **If NO**, spend time in prayer and let it go, continually laying it at the feet of Jesus.
   - **If YES**, ask:
2. Is there anything productive* I can do about it?   Yes ☐   No ☐
   (*Consider whether it has potential to repair the issue & whether I will look back on the action with regret.)
   - **If NO**, spend time in prayer and let it go, continually laying it at the feet of Jesus.
   - **If YES**, ask:
3. What can I do, and how can I do it ASAP or implement a long-term plan? _____
   _____
   _____

4. Spend time in prayer and let it go, continually laying it at the feet of Jesus.

My prayer for the day: _____
_____
_____
_____

Random things I'd like to talk about, process, or remember: _____
_____
_____
_____

Today I'm thankful for: _____
_____
_____

Anything about today that was:
True: _____
Honorable: _____
Pure: _____
Lovely: _____
Admirable: _____
Excellent: _____
Worthy of Praise: _____

A negative thought/lie I'm trying to retrain is: _____
_____
_____
_____

A Bible verse to teach myself the truth when that thought/lie arises is:
_____
_____
_____

A song, Bible verse, or quote I'm going to ponder throughout the day is:
_____
_____
_____

Successes, progress, or things I learned today: _____
_____
_____

A negative emotion I battled today was: _____

1. Was it appropriate to the situation*?  Yes ☐  No ☐
   (*Consider whether it was a real issue or influenced by mood, circumstance, or prior events.)
   - **If NO**, spend time in prayer and let it go, continually laying it at the feet of Jesus.
   - **If YES**, ask:
2. Is there anything productive* I can do about it?  Yes ☐  No ☐
   (*Consider whether it has potential to repair the issue & whether I will look back on the action with regret.)
   - **If NO**, spend time in prayer and let it go, continually laying it at the feet of Jesus.
   - **If YES**, ask:
3. What can I do, and how can I do it ASAP or implement a long-term plan? _____
   _____
   _____

4. Spend time in prayer and let it go, continually laying it at the feet of Jesus.

My prayer for the day: _____
_____
_____
_____

Random things I'd like to talk about, process, or remember: _____
_____
_____

# Notes

# Not the End

While this is the last section, it's never the end. Your journey and mine will continue through the rest of our lives. There are more transformative truths I could write about even now, but this is where the Lord has told me to pause.

Each chapter covered a concept that pushed me further into contentment and out of dissatisfaction, into hope and out of despair, into confidence and out of insecurity, into faith and out of fear.

But it's likely that my faulty mindsets are different than yours. We all have a different framework, formation, and foundation.

Identify the thought patterns that induce dissatisfaction, despair, insecurity, and fear in your own life, and use the journal pages to retrain them into biblical truths that inspire the Lord's contentment, hope, confidence, and faith.

But if there's one faulty mindset we MUST overcome; that's the false belief that we *cannot* change.

Believing this sounds like we're being humble and self-deprecating, but implied in it is the idea that *God cannot change us.*

Are we "confident of this very thing, that He who began a good work among you will complete it by the day of Christ Jesus" (Philippians 1:6)?

God is the only one "with whom there is no variation or shifting shadow (James 1:17). He is the only one who "does not change" (Malachi 3:6).

The rest of us are moldable and will never stop changing in this lifetime. We can change for the good or the bad.

We choose. And not choosing—or not taking action—is a choice. We almost never get better by accident.

## Taking Every Thought Captive

We choose our attitudes by choosing to believe God's truth. We know that He cannot lie, so we start there.

If we know He cannot lie, then it follows we can trust everything He says.

We layer that over everything else we struggle with in life, and we must begin by choosing to believe what He says even when it doesn't feel true.

If obeying Him feels like it's depriving me of something good, I layer His Word over the top of it—"He withholds no good thing from those who walk with integrity" (Psalm 84:11).

If the evil I've experienced in my life feels hopeless and like nothing good could ever come out of it, I layer it with the fact that I "know that God causes all things to work together for good to those who love God, to those who are called according to His purpose" (Romans 8:28).

Since all His promises are already layered under believing the truth that God cannot lie, we must choose to believe these things or acknowledge the fact that somewhere deep down, we don't trust Him.

We don't, however, wallow in the disbelief feeling unworthy. We bring it straight to Him and, like the father in Mark 9:24, we cry out, "I do believe; help my unbelief!"

We give those thoughts to the Lord, casting our cares on Him once again, and we begin to take our thoughts captive and renew our minds by reminding ourselves of and training ourselves to believe truth.

The Lord already knows every last one of our unbelieving thoughts and feelings. He wants us to give them to Him; He wants to help heal them.

Be real with yourself and with God about where you are, but don't let yourself stay there. Renewing our minds isn't easy. It's difficult emotional work. It requires facing painful things in our pasts, being honest about things we don't like about ourselves, and accepting truths we don't always find comfortable.

But it's worth it. It leads to hope, freedom, contentment, and joy that cannot be taken away.

Start now. Start yesterday. The abundant life awaits.